FAST TALK AUDIO

Italian

D1155088

lonely planet

Fast Talk Audio Italian
1st edition – May 2007

Published by
Lonely Planet Publications Pty Ltd ABN 36 005 607 983
90 Maribyrnong St, Footscray, Victoria 3011, Australia

Lonely Planet Offices
Australia Locked Bag 1, Footscray, Victoria 3011
USA 150 Linden St, Oakland CA 94607
UK 72-82 Rosebery Ave, London, EC1R 4RW

Publishing Manager Chris Rennie
Commissioning Editor Rachel Williams
Project Manager Adam McCrow
Series Designer Yukiyoshi Kamimura
Layout Designer Katie Thuy Bui
Editors Vanessa Battersby, Branislava Vladisavljevic

Photography
Little baby Fiat by Jonathan Smith
© Lonely Planet Images 2007

ISBN 978 174179 207 2

text © Lonely Planet Publications Pty Ltd 2007

10 9 8 7 6 5 4 3 2

Printed by through Colorcraft Ltd, Hong Kong. Printed in China

LISTEN 5

Greetings, goodbyes
  & introductions 5
Background 5
Making conversation 6
Feelings 7
Getting around 7
Accommodation 7
Shopping 8

Photography 8
Going out 9
Sightseeing 9
Finding a place to eat/drink 10
Self-catering 10
Ordering food & drink 10
In the bar 11
Medical needs 11

CHAT 13

Meeting & greeting 13
Essentials 13
Breaking the language barrier ... 16
Personal details 17
Occupations & study 17

Age 18
Feelings 18
Beliefs 19
Weather 19

EXPLORE 20

Doing the sights 20
Gallery & museum hopping 21
Tours 22

Getting in 22
Top 5 day trips 24
Top 10 sights 25

SHOP 27

Essentials 27
Hot shop spots 28
Paying 29

Clothes & shoes 30
Books & music 30
Photography 32

ENJOY 33

What's on? 33
Meeting up 34

Small talk 34

CONTENTS

EAT & DRINK — 35

Choosing & booking 35
Eateries 36
Ordering 36
Nonalcoholic drinks 37
Caffè della casa 38
Alcoholic drinks 38
In the bar 39
Buying food 39
Special diets & allergies 40
On the menu 41
Menu decoder 42

SERVICES — 49

Post office 49
Bank 49
Phone 50
Mobile/cell phone 51
Internet 52

GO — 53

Directions 53
Getting around 54
Tickets & luggage 55
Bus, metro, taxi & train 57
Car & motorbike hire 59
Road signs 60

SLEEP — 61

Finding accommodation 61
Booking ahead & checking in 62
Requests & queries 63
Checking out 65

WORK — 66

Introductions 66
Business needs 67
After the deal 67

HELP — 68

Emergencies 68
Police 69
Health 70
Symptoms, conditions & allergies 71

LOOK UP — 74

Numbers 74
Colours 74
Times & dates 75
English–Italian dictionary 92
Italian–English dictionary 95

4

LISTEN

Welcome to *Listen* – the quickest way to chat like a local. This chapter will guide you through each of the 99 essential phrases listed on your Fast Talk Audio CD – just check inside the back cover! Plug in those headphones and follow along with the track listing below.

Greetings, goodbyes & introductions

track

1	Hello.	*Buongiorno.*
2	Goodbye.	*Arrivederci.*
3	How are you?	*Come sta?* pol
		Come stai? inf
4	Fine, and you?	*Bene, e Lei?* pol
		Bene, e tu? inf
5	My name is ...	*Mi chiamo ...*
6	Pleased to meet you.	*Piacere.*
7	This is my partner.	*Le presento il mio compagno.* m
		Le presento la mia compagna. f

Background

track

8	Where are you from?	*Da dove viene?* pol
		Da dove vieni? inf
9	I'm from ...	*Vengo da ...*
10	I'm married.	*Sono sposato.* m
		Sono sposata. f
11	I'm single.	*Sono celibe.* m
		Sono nubile. f

5

12 **What's your phone number?**
Qual'è il Suo numero di telefono? pol
Qual'è il tuo numero di telefono? inf

13 **What's your email address?**
Qual'è il Suo indirizzo di email? pol
Qual'è il tuo indirizzo di email? inf

Making conversation
track

14 **What's your occupation?**
Che lavoro fa? pol
Che lavoro fai? inf

15 **I'm an office worker.**
Sono n'impiegato. m
Sono n'impiegata. f

16 **I'm a manual worker.**
Sono manovale. m&f

17 **I'm a businessperson.**
Sono n'uomo d'affari. m
Sono na donna d'affari. f

18 **I'm a student.**
Sono no studente. m
Sono na studentessa. f

19 **I'm an artist.**
Sono n'artista. m&f

20 **How old are you?**
Quanti anni ha? pol
Quanti anni hai? inf

21 **I'm (25) years old.** *Ho (venticinque) anni.*

22 **Do you like art?** *Ti piace l'arte?*

23 **Do you like sport?** *Ti piace lo sport?*

24 **Do you like reading?** *Ti piace leggere?*

| 25 | Do you like to dance? | *Ti piace ballare?* |
| 26 | Do you like travelling? | *Ti piace viaggiare?* |

Feelings

track

27	I'm hungry.	*Ho fame.*
28	I'm cold.	*Ho freddo.*
29	I'm hot.	*Ho caldo.*
30	I'm thirsty.	*Ho sete.*
31	Are you okay?	*Sta bene?/Stai bene?* pol/inf

Getting around

track

32	Is this the bus (to Venice)?	*È questo l'autobus (per Venezia)?*
33	Is this the plane (to Venice)?	*È questo l'aereo (per Venezia)?*
34	Is this the train (to Venice)?	*È questo il treno (per Venezia)?*
35	How much is it (to Rome)?	*Quant'è (per Roma)?*
36	Is this taxi available?	*È libero questo tassì?*
37	What time does it leave?	*A che ora parte?*
38	Where's the city centre?	*Dov'è il centro città?*
39	Where's the hotel?	*Dov'è l'albergo?*
40	Where's the market?	*Dov'è il mercato?*

Accommodation

track

41	Is there a camp site nearby?	
	C'è un campeggio più vicino?	
42	Can you recommend somewhere cheap?	
	Può consigliare qualche posto economico?	
43	Can you recommend somewhere good?	
	Può consigliare qualche posto buono?	

44 **How much is it per night?**
Quanto costa per una notte?

45 **I'd like to book a room, please.**
Vorrei prenotare una camera, per favore.

Shopping
track

46 **Where's the supermarket?**
Dov'è il supermercato?

47 **Where's a bank?**
Dov'è la banca?

48 **Where can I buy (a padlock)?**
Dove posso comprare (un lucchetto)?

49 **Can I look at it?**
Posso dare un'occhiata?

50 **What's your lowest price?**
Qual'è Suo prezzo migliore?

51 **Can you write down the price?**
Può scrivere il prezzo?

52 **I'd like a receipt, please.**
Vorrei una ricevuta, per favore.

Photography
track

53 **I need a (200) speed film for this camera.**
*Vorrei un rullino da (duecento) ASA per
questa macchina fotografica.*

54 **I need an APS film for this camera.**
Vorrei un rullino da APS per questa macchina fotografica.

55 **I need a black and white film for this camera.**
*Vorrei un rullino in bianco e nero per
questa macchina fotografica.*

56 **Can you load my film?**
   Potrebbe inserire il mio rullino?

57 **Can you develop this film?**
   Potrebbe sviluppare questo rullino?

58 **When will it be ready?**
   Quando sarà pronto?

Going out
track

59 **I feel like going to the movies.**
   Ho voglia di andare al cinema.

60 **I feel like going to the theatre.**
   Ho voglia di andare a teatro.

61 **I feel like going to a concert.**
   Ho voglia di andare a un concerto.

62 **Where can I find clubs?**
   Dove sono dei clubs?

63 **Where can I find gay venues?**
   Dove sono dei locali gay?

64 **Where can I find pubs?**
   Dove sono dei pub?

Sightseeing
track

65 **When's the next day trip?**
   A che ora parte la prossima escursione in giornata?

66 **How long is the tour?**
   Quanto dura la gita?

67 **Is the admission charge included?**
   È incluso il prezzo d'ingresso?

68 **What time should we be back?**
   A che ora dovremmo ritornare?

LISTEN

9

Finding a place to eat/drink

track

69   **Can you recommend a restaurant?**
      Potrebbe consigliare un ristorante?

70   **Can you recommend a café?**
      Potrebbe consigliare un bar?

71   **Do you have vegetarian food?**
      Avete piatti vegetariani?

72   **Is there a vegetarian restaurant near here?**
      C'è un ristorante vegetariano qui vicino?

73   **I'd like a table for (four) please.**
      Vorrei un tavolo per (quattro), per favore.

74   **I'd like the nonsmoking section, please.**
      Vorrei la sezione è non fumatori, per favore.

75   **Can you recommend a bar?**
      Potrebbe consigliare un locale?

Self-catering

track

76   **How much is (a kilo)?**   *Quanto costa (un chilo)?*
77   **I'd like (100 grams).**   *Vorrei (un etto).*
78   **I'd like (six) slices.**   *Vorrei (sei) fette.*
79   **What's the local speciality?**   *Qual'è la specialità di questa regione?*

Ordering food & drink

track

80   **I'd like to see the drinks list, please.**
      Vorrei la lista delle bevande, per favore.

81   **I'd like the menu, please.**
      Vorrei il menù, per favore.

82	What would you recommend?	*Cosa mi consiglia?*
83	A cup of coffee (with milk).	*Un caffè (con latte).*
84	A cup of tea (with milk).	*Un tè (con latte).*
85	I'd like the bill, please.	*Vorrei il conto, per favore.*

In the bar
track

86	What would you like?	*Cosa prendi?*
87	I'll buy you a drink.	*Ti offro da bere.*
88	A glass of beer.	*Un bicchiere di birra.*
89	A glass of white wine.	*Un bicchiere di vino bianco.*
90	A glass of red wine.	*Un bicchiere di vino rosso.*
91	Champagne.	*Champagne.*
92	Cheers!	*Salute!*

Medical needs
track

93	Help! *Aiuto!*
94	I need a doctor who speaks English.
	Ho bisogno di un medico che parli inglese.
95	Could I see a female doctor?
	Posso vedere una dottoressa?
96	I've run out of my medication.
	Ho finito la mia medicina.
97	Where's the nearest dentist?
	Dov'è al dentista più vicino?
98	Where's the nearest hospital?
	Dov'è l'ospedale più vicino?
99	Where's the nearest night pharmacy?
	Dov'è la farmacia di turno più vicina?

LISTEN

Language name: Italian

Italian is known to its native speakers as *italiano* ee·tal·*ya*·no.

Language family: Romance

Italian belongs to the Romance family of languages and is a close relative of
Spanish, French, Portuguese and Romanian.

Key country & secondary countries:

The key country where Italian is spoken is of course Italy, but Italian is
also spoken by minorities in Switzerland, Slovenia, France and the Istrian
peninsula of Croatia where the language has official status.

Approximate number of speakers:

Nearly 65 million people speak Italian worldwide. Many of those who live in
Italy also speak a dialect specific to their native region.

Donations to English:

English speakers will recognise many Italian words related to music, cuisine
and art. Opera, virtuoso, broccoli, spaghetti and fresco are just a few.

Grammar:

The structure of Italian holds no major surprises for English speakers due to
the common Latin ancestry of the two languages.

Pronunciation:

With the exception of the rolled *r*, the sounds of Italian can almost all be
found in English. You'll be surprised how easy it is to pronounce Italian words.

Abbreviations used in this book:

m	masculine	sg	singular	pol	polite
f	feminine	pl	plural	inf	informal

CHAT
Meeting & greeting

Hello.	*Buongiorno/Salve.* pol	bwon·*jor*·no/*sal*·ve
Hi.	*Ciao.* inf	chow
Good morning/ afternoon.	*Buongiorno.*	bwon·*jor*·no
Good evening.	*Buonasera.*	bwo·na·*se*·ra
Good night.	*Buonanotte.*	bwo·na·*no*·te
Goodbye.	*Arrivederci.* pol	a·ree·ve·*der*·chee
Bye.	*Ciao.* inf	chow
Mr/Sir	*Signore*	see·*nyo*·re
Mrs/Madam	*Signora*	see·*nyo*·ra
Miss/Ms	*Signorina*	see·nyo·*ree*·na
Doctor	*Dottore/Dottoressa* m/f	do·*to*·re/do·to·*re*·sa

Essentials

Yes.	*Sì.*	see
No.	*No.*	no
Please.	*Per favore.*	per fa·*vo*·re
Thank you (very much).	*Grazie (mille).*	*gra*·tsye (*mee*·le)
You're welcome.	*Prego.*	*pre*·go
Excuse me.	*Mi scusi.* pol	mee *skoo*·zee
	Scusami. inf	*skoo*·za·mee
Sorry.	*Mi dispiace.*	mee dees·*pya*·che

13

How are you?
> *Come sta?* pol — *ko·me sta*
> *Come stai?* inf — *ko·me stai*

Fine. And you?
> *Bene. E Lei/tu?* pol/inf — *be·ne e lay/too*

What's your name?
> *Come si chiama?* pol — *ko·me see kya·ma*
> *Come ti chiami?* inf — *ko·me tee kya·mee*

My name is ...
> *Mi chiamo ...* — mee *kya·mo* ...

I'd like to introduce you to ...
> *Le/Ti presento ...* pol/inf — le/tee pre·*zen*·to ...

I'm pleased to meet you.
> *Piacere.* — pya·*che*·re

It's been great meeting you.
> *È stato veramente un* — e *sta*·to ve·ra·*men*·te oon
> *piacere conoscerla/* — pya·*che*·re ko·*no*·sher·la/
> *conoscerti.* pol/inf — ko·*no*·sher·tee

This is my ...	*Le/Ti presento ...* pol/inf	le/tee pre·*zen*·to ...
colleague	*il mio collega* m	eel *mee*·o ko·*le*·ga
	la mia collega f	la *mee*·a ko·*le*·ga
friend	*il mio amico* m	eel *mee*·o a·*mee*·ko
	la mia amica f	la *mee*·a a·*mee*·ka
husband	*mio marito*	*mee*·o ma·*ree*·to
partner	*il mio*	eel *mee*·o
(intimate)	*compagno* m	kom·*pa*·nyo
	la mia	la *mee*·a
	compagna f	kom·*pa*·nya
wife	*mia moglie*	*mee*·a mo·lye

I'm here ...	*Sono qui ...*	*so*·no kwee ...
for a holiday	*in vacanza*	een va·*kan*·tsa
on business	*per affari*	per a·*fa*·ree
to study	*per motivi*	per mo·*tee*·vee
	di studio	dee *stoo*·dyo
with my family	*con la mia*	kon la *mee*·a
	famiglia	fa·*mee*·lya
with my partner	*con il mio*	kon eel *mee*·o
	compagno m	kom·*pa*·nyo
	con la mia	kon la *mee*·a
	compagna f	kom·*pa*·nya

How long are you here for?

Quanto tempo si fermerà? pol kwan·to *tem*·po see fer·me·*ra*
Quanto tempo ti fermerai? inf kwan·to *tem*·po tee fer·me·*rai*

I'm here for ... days/weeks.

Sono qui per ... giorni/ *so*·no kwee per ... *jor*·nee/
settimane. se·tee·*ma*·ne

For numbers see the box feature in **LOOK UP**, page 74.

Here's my ...	*Ecco il mio ...*	e·ko eel *mee*·o ...
What's your ...?	*Qual'è il Suo/*	kwa·*le* eel *soo*·o/
	tuo ...?	*too*·o ...
address	*indirizzo*	een·dee·*ree*·tso
email address	*indirizzo di*	een·dee·*ree*·tso dee
	email	e·mayl
fax number	*numero di fax*	*noo*·me·ro dee faks
home number	*numero di casa*	*noo*·me·ro dee *ka*·za
mobile number	*numero di*	*noo*·me·ro dee
	cellulare	che·loo·*la*·re
work number	*numero di*	*noo*·me·ro dee
	lavoro	la·*vo*·ro

15

Breaking the language barrier

Do you speak English?
Parla inglese?   *par*·la een·*gle*·ze

Does anyone speak English?
C'è qualcuno che parla   che kwal·*koo*·no ke *par*·la
inglese?   een·*gle*·ze

Do you understand?
Capisce?   ka·*pee*·she

I understand.
Capisco.   ka·*pee*·sko

I don't understand.
Non capisco.   non ka·*pee*·sko

I speak a little.
Parlo un po'.   *par*·lo oon po

What does 'vietato' mean?
Che cosa vuol dire 'vietato'?   ke *ko*·za vwol *dee*·re vye·*ta*·to

How do you ...?	*Come si ...?*	*ko*·me see ...
pronounce this	*pronuncia*	pro·*noon*·cha
	questo	*kwe*·sto
write 'arrivederci'	*scrive*	*skree*·ve
	'arrivederci'	a·ree·ve·*der*·chee

Could you	*Può ... per*	pwo ... per
please ...?	*favore?*	fa·*vo*·re
repeat that	*ripeterlo*	ree·*pe*·ter·lo
speak more	*parlare più*	par·*la*·re pyoo
slowly	*lentamente*	len·ta·*men*·te
write it down	*scriverlo*	*skree*·ver·lo

Personal details

Where are you from?
   Da dove viene/vieni? pol/inf   da *do*·ve *vye*·ne/*vye*·nee

I'm from ...	*Vengo ...*	*ven*·go ...
England	*dall'Inghilterra*	da·leen·geel·*te*·ra
New Zealand	*dalla Nuova*	*da*·la *nwo*·va
	Zelanda	ze·*lan*·da
the USA	*dagli Stati*	*da*·lyee *sta*·tee
	Uniti	oo·*nee*·tee

I'm ...	*Sono ...*	*so*·no ...
married	*sposato/a* m/f	spo·*za*·to/a
separated	*separato/a* m/f	se·pa·*ra*·to/a
single (man)	*celibe*	*che*·lee·be
single (woman)	*nubile*	*noo*·bee·le

Occupations & study

What's your occupation?
   Che lavoro fa/fai? pol/inf   ke la·*vo*·ro fa/fai

I'm a/an ...	*Sono ...*	*so*·no ...
manual worker	*manovale* m&f	ma·no·*va*·le
office worker	*impiegato/a* m/f	eem·pye·*ga*·to/a
tradesperson	*operaio/a* m/f	o·pe·*ra*·yo/a

I'm ...	*Sono ...*	*so*·no ...
retired	*pensionato/a* m/f	pen·syo·*na*·to/a
unemployed	*disoccupato/a* m/f	dee·zo·koo·*pa*·to/a

I work in ...	Lavoro nel campo ...	la·*vo*·ro nel *kam*·po ...
administration	dell'amministra-	de·la·mee·nee·stra·
	zione	*tsyo*·ne
public relations	delle relazioni	de·le re·la·*tsyo*·nee
	pubbliche	poo·*blee*·ke
retail	della vendità	de·la ven·dee·*ta*
	al minuto	al mee·*noo*·to
I'm studying ...	Sto studiando ...	sto stoo·*dyan*·do ...
arts/humanities	lettere	*le*·te·re
business	commercio	ko·*mer*·cho
engineering	ingegneria	een·je·nye·*ree*·a

Age

How old ...?	Quanti anni ...?	kwan·tee *a*·nee ...
are you	ha/hai pol/inf	a/ai
is your son	ha Suo figlio	a *soo*·o *fee*·lyo
is your daughter	ha Sua figlia	a *soo*·a *fee*·lya

| I'm ... years old. | | |
| Ho ... anni. | | o ... *a*·nee |

For your age, see the box feature in **LOOK UP**, page 74.

Feelings

I'm ...	Ho ...	o ...
I'm not ...	Non ho ...	non o ...
Are you ...?	Ha/Hai ...? pol/inf	a/ai ...
cold	freddo	*fre*·do
hungry	fame	*fa*·me
sleepy	sonno	*so*·no

I'm ...	Sono ...	so·no ...
I'm not ...	Non sono ...	non so·no ...
Are you ...?	È/Sei ...? pol/inf	e/say ...
embarrassed	imbarazzato/a m/f	eem·ba·ra·tsa·to/a
happy	felice	fe·lee·che
worried	preoccupato/a m/f	pre·o·koo·pa·to/a

Beliefs

I'm ...	Sono ...	so·no ...
I'm not ...	Non sono ...	non so·no ...
atheist	ateo/a m/f	a·te·o/a
Buddhist	buddista	boo·dee·sta
Catholic	cattolico/a m/f	ka·to·lee·ko/a
Christian	cristiano/a m/f	krees·tya·no/a
Hindu	indù	een·doo
Jewish	ebreo/a m/f	e·bre·o/a
Muslim	musulmano/a m/f	moo·sool·ma·no/a
religious	religioso/a m/f	re·lee·jo·zo/a

Weather

What's the weather like?

Che tempo fa?		ke tem·po fa

It's ...	Fa ...	fa ...
cold	freddo	fre·do
(very) hot	(molto) caldo	(mol·to) kal·do
warm	bel tempo	bel tem·po

It's ...		
freezing	Si gela.	see je·la
rainy	Piove.	pyo·ve
windy	Tira vento.	tee·ra ven·to

19

EXPLORE
Doing the sights

What would you do if you only had one day?
Lei che farebbe se avesse   lay ke fa·*re*·be se a·*ve*·se
solo una giornata?   *so*·lo *oo*·na jor·*na*·ta

Do you have information on local sights?
Avete delle informazioni   a·*ve*·te *de*·le een·for·ma·*tsyo*·nee
su posti locali?   soo *pos*·tee lo·*ka*·lee

I'd like to see ...
Vorrei vedere ...   vo·*ray* ve·*de*·re ...

I have only (one day).
Ho solo (un giorno).   o *so*·lo (oon *jor*·no)

What sights should I definitely see?
Quali posti dovrei   *kwa*·lee *pos*·tee do·*vray*
assolutamente vedere?   a·so·loo·ta·*men*·te ve·*de*·re

What's that?
Cos'è?   ko·*ze*

Who made it?
Chi l'ha fatto?   kee la *fa*·to

How old is it?
Quanti anni ha?   *kwan*·tee *a*·nee a

I'd like a/an ...	*Vorrei ...*	vo·*ray* ...
audio set	*un auricolare*	oo·now·ree·ko·*la*·re
catalogue	*un catalogo*	oon ka·*ta*·lo·go
guide	*una guida*	*oo*·na *gwee*·da
guidebook in	*una guida*	*oo*·na *gwee*·da
English	*in inglese*	een een·*gle*·ze
local map	*una cartina*	*oo*·na kar·*tee*·na
	della zona	*de*·la *dzo*·na

Could you take a photograph of me?
Può farmi una foto?   pwo *far*·mee *oo*·na *fo*·to

Can I take a photograph?
Posso fare una foto?   po·so *fa*·re *oo*·na *fo*·to

I'll send you the photograph.
Le spedirò la foto.   le spe·dee·*ro* la *fo*·to

Gallery & museum hopping

When's the ... open?   *A che ora apre ...?*   a ke *o*·ra *a*·pre ...
   gallery   *la galleria*   la ga·le·*ree*·a
   museum   *il museo*   eel moo·*ze*·o

What's in the collection?
Quali sono le opere   kwa·lee *so*·no le *o*·pe·re
qui esposte?   kwee es·*pos*·te

It's an exhibition of ...
È una mostra di ...   e *oo*·na *mos*·tra dee ...

I like the works of ...
Mi piacciono le opere di ...   mee *pya*·cho·no le *o*·pe·re dee ...

It reminds me of ...
Mi ricorda ...   mee ree·*kor*·da ...

... art   *l'arte ...*   *lar*·te ...
   byzantine   *bizantina*   bee·dzan·*tee*·na
   futurist   *futurista*   foo·too·*ree*·sta
   Gothic   *gotica*   *go*·tee·ka
   Renaissance   *rinascimentale*   ree·na·shee·men·*ta*·le
   Romanesque   *romanica*   ro·*ma*·nee·ka

Getting in

What's the admission charge?
Quant'è il prezzo   kwan·*te* eel *pre*·tso
d'ingresso?   deen·*gre*·so

It costs (seven euros).
Costa (sette Euro).   *kos*·ta (*se*·te e·*oo*·ro)

What time does it open?
A che ora apre?   a ke *o*·ra *a*·pre

What time does it close?
A che ora chiude?   a ke *o*·ra *kyoo*·de

Is there a discount for ...?	*C'è uno sconto per ...?*	che *oo*·no *skon*·to per ...
children	*bambini*	bam·*bee*·nee
families	*famiglie*	fa·*mee*·lye
groups	*gruppi*	*groo*·pee
pensioners	*pensionati*	pen·syo·*na*·tee
students	*studenti*	stoo·*den*·tee

Tours

Can you recommend a ...?	*Può consigliare...?*	pwo kon·see·*lya*·re...
boat trip	*una gita in barca*	*oo*·na *jee*·ta een *bar*·ka
day trip	*un'escursione in giornata*	oo·nes·koor·*syo*·ne een jor·*na*·ta
tour	*una gita turistica*	*oo*·na *jee*·ta too·*ree*·stee·ka

When's the next ...?	*A che ora parte la prossima ...?*	a ke *o*·ra *par*·te la *pro*·see·ma ...
boat trip	*gita in barca*	*jee*·ta een *bar*·ka
day trip	*escursione in giornata*	es·koor·*syo*·ne een jor·*na*·ta
tour	*gita turistica*	*jee*·ta too·ree·stee·ka

Is ... included?	*È incluso ...?*	e een·*kloo*·zo ...
accommodation	*l'alloggio*	la·*lo*·jo
the admission charge	*il prezzo d'ingresso*	eel *pre*·tso deen·*gre*·so
food	*il vitto*	eel *vee*·to
transport	*il trasporto*	eel tras·*por*·to

Do I need to take ... with me?
Devo portare ... con me?   •   *de*·vo por·*ta*·re ... kon me

The guide will pay.
La guida pagherà.   •   la *gwee*·da pa·ge·*ra*

The guide has paid.
La guida ha pagato.   •   la *gwee*·da a pa·*ga*·to

How long is the tour?
Quanto dura la gita?   •   *kwan*·to *doo*·ra la *jee*·ta

What time should we be back?
A che ora dovremmo ritornare?   •   a ke *o*·ra dov·*re*·mo ree·tor·*na*·re

I'm with them.
Sono con loro.   •   *so*·no kon *lo*·ro

I've lost my group.
Ho perso il mio gruppo.   •   o *per*·so eel *mee*·o *groo*·po

Have you seen a group of (Australians)?
Ha visto un gruppo di (australiani)?   •   a *vees*·to oon *groo*·po dee (ows·tra·*lya*·nee)

Top 5 day trips

Sometimes the frenzied pace of Italian cities can get a little overwhelming. For a more relaxing alternative, head out of town to enjoy a quieter, off-the-beaten-track cultural experience.

Top day trip excursions from Rome:

Ostia Antica
os·tee·a an·tee·ka

These ruins of Rome's main port for six centuries provide a fascinating insight into a working Roman town. The deserted city was buried in a river of salt so the remains have been wonderfully well preserved.

Tivoli
tee·vo·lee

The hilltop town of Tivoli was once a popular suburban retreat for prominent Romans. Spend the morning touring the sumptuous Villa Adriana, replete with a fishpond, barracks and temples. In the afternoon you can picnic in the stunning gardens of the Villa d'Este, a pleasure palace built in the mid-16th century.

Top day trip excursions from Florence:

Chianti
kyan·tee

Situated in one of the world's most famous wine regions, the surrounding scenery features castles, villages and villas perched picturesquely on hilltops. Don't leave without visiting a winery and tasting some of Chianti's world-famous wine.

Lucca
loo·ka

Lucca is an excellent place to escape the hustle and bustle of Florence. Check out the dazzling Romanesque church of San Michele and admire the strikingly resplendent mosaic in the church of San Frediano.

Siena
sye·na

Set on three hills and flanked by fertile valleys, Siena is a charming city of medieval turrets and towers. Take a stroll around the magnificent 14th-century piazza in the centre of town.

Top 10 sights

From the sultry south to the metropolitan north, Italy flaunts its many centuries of glorious history. It would take a lifetime to explore all the wonders of Italy's fascinating past, but if you don't have that much time on your hands, make sure you pack in a few of these famous highlights:

Pompeii
pom·*pay*

This world-famous archaeological site near **Naples** is rightly Italy's most popular tourist attraction. Buried after the eruption of Mt Vesuvius in AD 79, the Roman town is still being excavated stone by stone. Spend a day wandering through the Roman streets and let your imagination unfold.

Il Colosseo
eel ko·lo·*say*·o

Once a venue for gory battles between beasts, slaves and gladiators, the Colosseum has become a symbol of **Rome** itself. In its day it could accommodate a staggering 50,000 spectators.

La Città del Vaticano
la chee·*ta* del va·tee·*ka*·no

A must-see for any visitor to **Rome**, the Vatican City is dominated by St Peter's Basilica, a breath-taking structure designed chiefly by Michelangelo. The extensive Vatican museum – boasting magnificent art and curiosities – leads to the Sistine Chapel. Arrive early to beat the crowds.

La Torre Pendente di Pisa
la *to*·re pen·*den*·te dee *pee*·sa

Perhaps the world's most famous architectural disaster, the Leaning Tower of **Pisa** is a sight to behold. The tower is now secure to climb, after a recent 12-year project to prevent it from toppling over completely.

Il Duomo di Firenze
eel *dwo*·mo dee fee·*ren*·tse

Built to show off the wealth and supremacy of Tuscany, the *Duomo* sits impressively in the centre of **Florence**, its marvellous terracotta-coloured dome towering above the surrounding buildings. Climb the adjacent bell tower for an unbeatable panoramic view of the city.

Il Ponte Vecchio
eel pon·te ve·kyo

Situated in **Florence** on the narrowest point of the river Arno, the *Ponte Vecchio* is a romantic place to visit by day or night. The bridge was once crowded with tanneries and butchers until the 16th century when they were replaced with decorous jewellers that continue to ply their trade here today.

Gli Uffizi
lyee oo·fee·tsee

You'll have to get up very early to avoid a long queue for the *Uffizi* in **Florence** but it's well worth the effort. Drift from room to room gazing at Italy's extraordinary artistic legacy. Even those with little knowledge of art will recognise Botticelli's famous *Birth of Venus* and Titian's *Venus of Urbino* – just two of the hundreds of stunning works on display.

La Basilica di San Marco
la ba·see·lee·ka dee san mar·ko

Towering imposingly over the *Piazza San Marco*, this grand basilica in **Venice** embodies a magnificent blend of decorative styles. The basilica's diverse architectural influences – ranging from Byzantine to Romanesque, Gothic and Renaissance – point to Venice's unique cosmopolitanism, still in evidence today. The inside of the building is adorned with an incredible array of treasures plundered from the East.

Il Duomo di Milano
eel dwo·mo dee mee·la·no

This massive cathedral is the centrepiece of **Milan**, a Gothic colossus that took over four hundred years to complete. The roof and the facade alone are crammed with 135 spires and 3200 statues.

La Scala
la ska·la

The famous opera house of **Milan** with its towering rows of curtained boxes is perhaps one of the most romantic places to experience some of Europe's finest musical talent. If you can't get tickets to the opera at this superb theatre, make sure you visit the enjoined museum which is full of musical oddities such as the plaster cast of Chopin's hands. Admission includes a peep at the theatre's auditorium.

SHOP
Essentials

Where's ... ?	Dov'è ... ?	do·ve ...
a bank	una banca	oo·na ban·ka
a cake shop	una	oo·na
	pasticceria	pa·stee·che·ree·a
a supermarket	un supermercato	oon soo·per·mer·ka·to

Where can I buy ...?
Dove posso comprare ...?   do·ve po·so kom·pra·re ...

I'd like to buy ...
Vorrei comprare ...   vo·ray kom·pra·re ...

Do you have any others?
Ne avete altri?   ne a·ve·te al·tree

Can I look at it?
Posso dare un'occhiata?   po·so da·re oo·no·kya·ta

I'm just looking.
Sto solo guardando.   sto so·lo gwar·dan·do

Could I have it wrapped, please?
Può incartarlo   pwo een·kar·tar·lo
per favore?   per fa·vo·re

Does it have a guarantee?
Ha la garanzia?   a la ga·ran·tsee·a

Can I have it sent overseas?
Può spedirlo all'estero?   pwo spe·deer·lo a·les·te·ro

Can I pick it up later?
Posso ritirarlo più tardi?   po·so ree·tee·rar·lo pyoo tar·dee

It's faulty/broken.
È difettoso/rotto.   e dee·fe·to·zo/ro·to

I'd like ..., please.	*Vorrei ..., per favore.*	vo·ray ... per fa·vo·re
my change	*il mio resto*	eel mee·o res·to
my money back	*un rimborso*	oon reem·bor·so
to change this	*cambiare questo*	kam·bya·re kwe·sto
to return this	*restituire*	res·tee·twee·re
	questo	kwe·sto

Hot shop spots

When good shoppers die they go to Italy, a veritable paradise of great spending options. If your wallet is starting to weigh you down, you can quickly lighten it at these renowned shopping locations:

Piazza di Spagna, Rome fi major fashion labels · accessories · jewellery · homeware

Via del Governo Vecchio, Rome fi second-hand clothes · upcoming Roman designs

Via dei Coronari, Via Margutta, Rome fi antiques · art · unusual souvenirs

Medieval Core, Florence – designer clothes · shoes · jewellery

Oltrano, Florence – local crafts · art

San Polo, Venice fi carnavale masks · costumes · ceramics · model gondolas

North of Piazza San Marco, Venice fi clothing · shoes · accessories

Golden Quad, Milan – expensive designer clothes · accessories · leather shoes · jewellery

Paying

How much is it?
Quant'è? kwan·*te*

Can you write down the price?
Può scrivere il prezzo? pwo *skree*·ve·re eel *pre*·tso

Can I have smaller notes?
Mi può dare banconote mee pwo *da*·re ban·ko·*no*·te
più piccole? pyoo *pee*·ko·le

That's too expensive.
È troppo caro. e *tro*·po *ka*·ro

Can you lower the price?
Può farmi lo sconto? pwo *far*·mee lo *skon*·to

Do you have something cheaper?
Ha qualcosa di a kwal·*ko*·za dee
meno costoso? *me*·no kos·*to*·zo

Do you accept ...?	*Accettate ...?*	a·che·*ta*·te ...
credit cards	*la carta di credito*	la *kar*·ta dee *kre*·dee·to
debit cards	*la carta di debito*	la *kar*·ta dee *de*·bee·to
travellers cheques	*gli assegni di viaggio*	lyee a·*se*·nyee dee vee·*a*·jo

I'd like ..., please.	*Vorrei ..., per favore.*	vo·*ray* ... per fa·*vo*·re
a receipt	*una ricevuta*	*oo*·na ree·che·*voo*·ta
my change	*il mio resto*	eel *mee*·o *res*·to
my money back	*un rimborso*	oon reem·*bor*·so

For phrases about banking, see **SERVICES**, page 49.

SHOP

29

Clothes & shoes

I'm looking for ...	*Sto cercando ...*	sto cher·*kan*·do ...
jeans	*dei jeans*	day jeens
shoes	*delle scarpe*	de·le *skar*·pe
underwear	*della biancheria*	de·la byan·ke·*ree*·a
	intima	een·tee·ma

Can I try it on?
Potrei provarmelo?   po·*tray* pro·*var*·me·lo

My size is (42).
Sono una taglia   so·no *oo*·na *ta*·lya
(quarantadue).   (kwa·*ran*·ta·*doo*·e)

It doesn't fit.
Non va bene.   non va *be*·ne

small	*piccola*	*pee*·ko·la
medium	*media*	*me*·dya
large	*forte*	*for*·te

It's too ...	*È troppo ...*	e *tro*·po
big	*grande*	*gran*·de
small	*piccolo*	*pee*·ko·lo
tight	*stretto*	*stre*·to

Books & music

Is there an English-language bookshop?
C'è una libreria   che *oo*·na lee·bre·*ree*·a
specializzata in   spe·cha·lee·*dza*·ta een
lingua inglese?   *leen*·gwa een·*gle*·ze

Is there an English-language section?
C'è una sezione di   che *oo*·na se·*tsyo*·ne dee
lingua inglese?   *leen*·gwa een·*gle*·ze

Do you have a/an ...	Avete ...	a·ve·te
book by ...	un libro di ...	oon lee·bro dee ...
entertainment guide	una guida agli spettacoli	oo·na gwee·da a·lyee spe·ta·ko·lee

I'd like a ...	Vorrei ...	vo·ray ...
map (city)	una pianta della città	oo·na pyan·ta de·la chee·ta
map (road)	una cartina stradale	oo·na kar·tee·na stra·da·le
newspaper (in English)	un giornale (in inglese)	oon jor·na·le (een een·gle·ze)
pen	una penna	oo·na pe·na
postcard	una cartolina	oo·na kar·to·lee·na

I'd like (a) ...	Vorrei ...	vo·ray ...
blank tape	una cassetta vuota	oo·na ka·se·ta vwo·ta
CD	un cidì	oon chee·dee
headphones	delle cuffia	de·le koo·fya

I'm looking for a CD by ...
Sto cercando un cidì di ...
sto cher·kan·do un chee·dee dee ...

I heard a group called ...
Ho sentito un gruppo chiamato ...
o sen·tee·to oon groo·po kya·ma·to ...

What's his/her best recording?
Qual'è la sua migliore incisione?
kwa·le la soo·a mee·lyo·re een·chee·zyo·ne

Can I listen to it here?
Potrei ascoltarlo qui?
po·tray as·kol·tar·lo kwee

Photography

English	Italian	Pronunciation
I need a/an ...	Vorrei un rullino	vo·*ray* oon roo·*lee*·no
film for this	... per questa	... per *kwe*·sta
camera.	macchina	*ma*·kee·na
	fotografica.	fo·to·*gra*·fee·ka
APS	da APS	da a·pee·*e*·se
B&W	in bianco e nero	een *byan*·ko e *ne*·ro
colour	a colori	a *ko*·lo·ree
(200) speed	da (duecento)	da (*doo*·e *chen*·to)
	ASA	*a*·za
Could you ...?	Potrebbe ...?	po·*tre*·be ...
develop this	sviluppare	svee·loo·*pa*·re
film	questo rullino	*kwe*·sto roo·*lee*·no
load my film	inserire il	een·se·*ree*·re eel
	mio rullino	*mee*·o roo·*lee*·no

How much is it to develop this film?
Quanto costa sviluppare   *kwan*·to *kos*·ta svee·loo·*pa*·re
questo rullino?   *kwe*·sto roo·*lee*·no

When will it be ready?
Quando sarà pronto?   *kwan*·do sa·*ra* pron·to

Do you have one-hour processing?
Si offre il servizio   see *o*·fre eel ser·*vee*·tsyo
sviluppo e stampa in   svee·*loo*·po e *stam*·pa een
un ora?   oon *o*·ra

I'm not happy with these photos.
Non mi piacciono   non mee *pya*·cho·no
queste foto.   *kwe*·ste *fo*·to

ENJOY
What's on?

What's on …?	Che c'è in programma …?	ke che een pro·gra·ma …
locally	in zona	een dzo·na
this weekend	questo fine settimana	kwe·sto fee·ne se·tee·ma·na
today	oggi	o·jee
tonight	stasera	sta·se·ra

Where are the …?	Dove sono …?	do·ve so·no …
clubs	dei clubs	day kloob
gay hangouts	dei locali gay	day lo·ka·lee gei
places to eat	i posti in cui mangiare	ee pos·tee een koo·ee man·ja·re
pubs	dei pub	day poob

Is there a local … guide?	C'è una guida … in questa città?	che oo·na gwee·da … een kwe·sta chee·ta
entertainment	agli spettacoli	a·lyee spe·ta·ko·lee
film	ai film	ai feelm

I feel like going to …	Ho voglia d'andare …	o vo·lya dan·da·re …
the ballet	a un balletto	a oon ba·le·to
a bar	a un locale	a oon lo·ka·le
a café	a un bar	a oon bar
a concert	a un concerto	a oon kon·cher·to
a nightclub	in un locale notturno	een oon lo·ka·le no·toor·no
the opera	all'opera	a·lo·pe·ra
a restaurant	in un ristorante	een oon rees·to·ran·te
the theatre	a teatro	a te·a·tro

ENJOY

33

Meeting up

What time shall we meet?
A che ora ci vediamo?   a ke *o*·ra chee ve·*dya*·mo

Where will we meet?
Dove ci vediamo?   *do*·ve chee ve·*dya*·mo

Let's meet at ...	*Incontriamoci ...*	een·kon·*trya*·mo·chee ...
(eight) o'clock	*alle (otto)*	*a*·le (*o*·to)
the entrance	*all'entrata*	a·len·*tra*·ta

Small talk

What do you do in your spare time?
Cosa fai nel tuo tempo   *ko*·za fai nel *too*·o tem·po
libero?   lee·be·ro

Do you like to ...?	*Ti piace ...?*	tee pya·che ...
I (don't) like to ...	*(Non) Mi piace ...*	(non) mee *pya*·che...
dance	*ballare*	ba·*la*·re
go to concerts	*andare ai*	an·*da*·re ai
	concerti	kon·*cher*·tee
listen to music	*ascoltare la*	as·kol·*ta*·re la
	musica	*moo*·zee·ka

I (don't) like ...	*(Non) mi piacciono ...*	(non) mee *pya*·cho·no ...
action movies	*i film d'azione*	ee feelm da·*tsyo*·ne
Italian films	*i film*	ee feelm
	italiani	ee·tal·*ya*·nee
sci-fi films	*i film di*	ee feelm dee
	fantascienza	fan·ta·*shen*·tsa

EAT & DRINK

breakfast	*prima colazione* f	pree·ma ko·la·*tsyo*·ne
lunch	*pranzo* m	*pran*·dzo
dinner	*cena* f	*che*·na
snack	*spuntino* m	spoon·*tee*·no

Choosing & booking

Where would you go for a celebration?
Dove andrebbe per   do·ve an·*dre*·be per
una celebrazione?   oo·na che·le·bra·*tsyo*·ne

Can you recommend a ...	*Potrebbe consigliare un ...*	po·*tre*·be kon·see·*lya*·re oon ...
bar	*locale*	lo·*ka*·le
café	*bar*	bar
restaurant	*ristorante*	rees·to·*ran*·te

Where would you go for ...?	*Dove andrebbe per ...*	do·ve an·*dre*·be per ...
a cheap meal	*un pasto economico*	oon *pas*·to e·ko·*no*·mee·ko
local specialities	*le specialità locali*	le spe·cha·lee·*ta* lo·*ka*·lee

I'd like ..., please.	*Vorrei ..., per favore.*	vo·*ray* ... per fa·*vo*·re
a table for (four)	*un tavolo per (quattro)*	oon *ta*·vo·lo per (*kwa*·tro)
the (non) smoking section	*(non) fumatori*	(non) foo·ma·*to*·ree

Eateries

With such a diverse selection of fantastic places to eat, you'll never go hungry in Italy. Sample the local flavour at some of these cheap and cheerful eateries:

bar/caffè bar/ka·*fe*
a café that serves drinks but also offers light meals such as bread rolls and snacks

osteria/trattoria os·te·*ree*·a/tra·to·*ree*·a
a local eatery providing simple food and regional specialities

paninoteca pa·nee·no·*te*·ka
a snack shop that serves delicious sandwiches made with cheese and cold meats

tavola calda ta·vo·la *kal*·da
a buffet offering local specialities, pizza, roasted meats and salads

pizzeria pee·tse·*ree*·a
a cheap restaurant specialising in pizza and calzoni (a folded pizza dish), usually prepared in a woodfired oven

ristorante ree·sto·*ran*·te
a sophisticated eatery – expect a high standard of service, a more expensive menu and an extensive winelist

Ordering

What would you recommend?
Cosa mi consiglia? *ko*·za mee kon·*see*·lya

I'd like …, please.	Vorrei …, per favore.	vo·*ray* … per fa·*vo*·re
the bill	il conto	eel *kon*·to
the menu	il menù	eel me·*noo*
the wine list	la lista dei vini	la *lee*·sta day *vee*·nee

I'd like ..., please.	Vorrei ..., per favore.	vo·*ray* ... per fa·*vo*·re
the chicken	il pollo	eel *po*·lo
a napkin	un tovagliolo	oon to·va·*lyo*·lo
pepper	il pepe	eel *pe*·pe
salt	il sale	eel *sa*·le
the set menu	il menù fisso	eel me·*noo* fee·so
I'd like it ...	Lo vorrei ...	lo vo·*ray* ...
medium	non troppo cotto	non *tro*·po *ko*·to
rare	al sangue	al *san*·gwe
well-done	ben cotto	ben *ko*·to
without sauce/	senza salsa/	*sen*·tsa *sal*·sa/
dressing	condimento	kon·dee·*men*·to

Nonalcoholic drinks

(cup of) coffee	(un) caffè m	(oon) ka·*fe*
(cup of) tea	(un) tè m	(oon) te
... with milk	... con latte	... kon *la*·te
... without/	... senza/con	... *sen*·tsa/kon
with (sugar)	(zucchero)	(*tsoo*·ke·ro)
orange juice (bottled)	succo m d'arancia	*soo*·ko da·*ran*·cha
orange juice (fresh)	spremuta f d'arancia	spre·*moo*·ta da·*ran*·cha
soft drink	bibita f	*bee*·bee·ta
... water	acqua f ...	*a*·kwa ...
hot	calda	*kal*·da
sparkling mineral	frizzante	free·*tsan*·te
still mineral	naturale	na·too·*ra*·le

Caffè della casa

Love the smell of coffee in the morning? Italy is a caffeine-addict's dream with more ways of making the humble brew than you can shake a spoon at:

caffè alla valdostana *ka·fe a·la val·dos·ta·na*
with grappa, lemon peel and spices

caffè americano *ka·fe a·me·ree·ka·no*
long and black

caffè corretto *ka·fe ko·re·to*
with a dash of liqueur

caffè doppio *ka·fe do·pyo*
long, strong and black

caffè macchiato *ka·fe ma·kya·to*
strong with a drop of milk

caffè ristretto *ka·fe ree·stre·to*
short, black and super strong

caffellate *ka·fe·la·te*
with milk – usually consumed at breakfast

cappuccino *ka·poo·chee·no*
prepared with milk, served with a lot of froth – considered a morning drink

espresso *es·pre·so*
short black

Alcoholic drinks

beer	*birra* f	*bee·ra*
brandy	*cognac* m	*ko·nyak*
champagne	*champagne* m	*sham·pa·nye*
cocktail	*cocktail* m	*kok·tayl*

a ... of beer	... di birra	... dee *bee*·ra
bottle	*una bottiglia*	*oo*·na bo·*tee*·lya
glass	*un bicchiere*	oon bee·*kye*·re

a bottle of	*una bottiglia*	*oo*·na bo·*tee*·lya
... wine	*di vino ...*	dee *vee*·no ...
a glass of	*un bicchiere*	oon bee·*kye*·re
... wine	*di vino ...*	dee *vee*·no ...
red	*rosso*	*ro*·so
sparkling	*spumante*	spoo·*man*·te
white	*bianco*	*byan*·ko

a shot of (whisky)
un sorso di (whisky)   oon *sor*·so dee (*wee*·skee)

In the bar

I'll have (a gin).	*Prendo (un gin).*	*pren*·do (oon jeen)
Same again, please.	*Un altro, per favore.*	oo·*nal*·tro per fa·*vo*·re
I'll buy you a drink.	*Ti offro da bere.*	tee *of*·ro da *be*·re
What would you like?	*Cosa prendi?*	*ko*·za *pren*·dee
It's my round.	*Offro io.*	*of*·ro *ee*·o
Cheers!	*Salute!*	sa·*loo*·te

Buying food

What's the local speciality?
Qual'è la specialità   kwa·*le* la spe·cha·lee·*ta*
di questa regione?   dee *kwe*·sta re·*jo*·ne

What's that?
Cos'è?   ko·*ze*

How much is (a kilo)?
Quanto costa (un chilo)?   kwan·to kos·ta (oon kee·lo)

I'd like some of that.
Mi piacerebbe un po' di quello.   mee pya·che·re·be oon po dee kwe·lo

I'd like some of those.
Vorrei un po' di quelli.   vo·ray oon po di kwe·lee

I'd like …	*Vorrei …*	vo·ray …
100g	*un etto*	oo·ne·to
(two) kilos	*(due) chili*	(doo·e) kee·lee
(three) pieces	*(tre) pezzi*	(tre) pe·tsee
(six) slices	*(sei) fette*	(say) fe·te

Enough, thanks.
Basta, grazie.   bas·ta gra·tsye

A bit more, please.
Un po' di più, per favore.   oon po dee pyoo per fa·vo·re

Less, please.
Meno, per favore.   me·no per fa·vo·re

Special diets & allergies

Is there a (vegetarian) restaurant near here?
C'è un ristorante
(vegetariano) qui vicino?
che oon rees·to·ran·te
(ve·je·ta·rya·no) kwee vee·chee·no

Do you have (vegetarian) food?
Avete piatti (vegetariani)?   a·ve·te pya·tee (ve·je·ta·rya·nee)

Could you prepare	*Potreste preparare*	po·tres·te pre·pa·ra·re
a meal without …?	*un pasto senza …?*	oon pas·to sen·tsa …
butter	*burro*	boo·ro
eggs	*uova*	wo·va
meat stock	*brodo di carne*	bro·do dee kar·ne

I'm ...	Sono ...	so·no ...
vegan	vegetaliano/a m/f	ve·je·ta·*lya*·no/a
vegetarian	vegetariano/a m/f	ve·je·ta·*rya*·no/a

I'm allergic to ...	Sono allergico/a ... m/f	so·no a·*ler*·jee·ko/a ...
caffeine	alla caffeina	*a*·la ka·fe·*yee*·na
dairy produce	ai latticini	ai la·tee·*chee*·nee
eggs	alle uova	*a*·le *wo*·va
gluten	al glutine	al *gloo*·tee·ne
nuts	alle noci	*a*·le *no*·chee
seafood	ai frutti di mare	ai *froo*·tee dee *ma*·re

For more on allergies see **HELP**, page 73 and **LOOK UP**, page 77.

On the menu

Antipasti	an·tee·*pas*·tee	appetisers
Zuppe	*tsoo*·pe	soups
Primi (piatti)	*pree*·mee (*pya*·tee)	entrees
Insalate	een·sa·*la*·te	salads
Secondi (piatti)	se·*kon*·dee (*pya*·tee)	main courses
Dolci	*dol*·chee	desserts
Bevande	be·*van*·de	drinks
Aperitivi	a·pe·ree·*tee*·vee	aperitifs
Liquori	lee·*kwo*·ree	spirits
Birre	*bee*·re	beers
Vini Frizzanti	*vee*·nee free·*tsan*·tee	sparkling wines
Vini Bianchi	*vee*·nee *byan*·kee	white wines
Vini Rossi	*vee*·nee *ro*·see	red wines
Vini da Dessert	*vee*·nee da de·*sert*	dessert wines

For more help reading the menu, see the **Menu decoder** on the next page.

Menu decoder

acciughe f pl	a·*choo*·ge	anchovies
aceto m	a·*che*·to	vinegar
affumicato/a m/f	a·foo·mee·*ka*·to/a	smoked
aglio m	*a*·lyo	garlic
agnello m	a·*nye*·lo	lamb
al dente	al *den*·te	'to the tooth' – describes cooked pasta & rice that are still slightly hard
al forno	al *for*·no	cooked in an oven
al sangue	al *san*·gwe	rare
al vapore	al va·*po*·re	steamed
alla diavola	a·la *dya*·vo·la	spicy dish
alla napoletana	a·la na·po·le·*ta*·na	from or in the style of Naples – usually includes tomatoes & garlic
all'amatriciana	al a·ma·tree·*cha*·na	spicy sauce with salami, tomato, capsicums & cheese
all'arrabbiata	al a·ra·*bya*·ta	'angry-style' – with spicy sauce
antipasto m	an·tee·*pas*·to	appetizers • hors d'oeuvres
aragosta f	a·ra·*go*·sta	lobster • crayfish
arancini m pl	a·ran·*chee*·nee	rice balls stuffed with a meat mixture
aringa f	a·*reen*·ga	herring
arista f	a·*ree*·sta	cured, cooked pork meat

aromi m pl	a·*ro*·mee	aromatic herbs • spices
babà m	ba·*ba*	dessert containing sultanas
baccalà m	ba·ka·*la*	dried salted cod
baci m pl	ba·chee	'kisses' – type of chocolate • type of pastry or biscuit
bagna f *cauda*	*ban*·ya *cow*·da	anchovy, olive oil & garlic dip served with raw vegetables
basilico m	ba·*zee*·lee·ko	basil
ben cotto/a m/f	ben *ko*·to/a	well done
besciamella f	be·sha·*me*·la	white sauce
bistecca f	bees·*te*·ka	steak
bollito/a m/f	bo·*lee*·to/a	boiled
braciola f	bra·*cho*·la	chop
brioche m	bree·*osh*	breakfast pastry
brodo m	*bro*·do	broth
bruschetta f	broos·*ke*·ta	toasted bread with olive oil & various toppings
budino m	boo·*dee*·no	milk-based pudding
busecca f	boo·ze·ka	tripe
cacciucco m	ka·*choo*·ko	seafood stew with wine, garlic & herbs
calzone m	kal·*tso*·ne	fried or baked flat bread made with two thin sheets of pasta stuffed with any number of ingredients
cannella f	ka·*ne*·la	cinnamon

cannelloni m pl	ka·ne·*lo*·nee	tubes of pasta stuffed with spinach, minced roast veal, ham, eggs, parmesan & spices
cantarelli m pl	kan·ta·*re*·lee	chanterelle mushrooms
cantucci m pl	kan·*too*·chee	crunchy, hard biscuits made with aniseed & almonds
caponata f	ka·po·*na*·ta	eggplant with a tomato sauce
carciofi m pl	kar·*cho*·fee	artichokes
ciabatta f	cha·*ba*·ta	crisp, flat & long bread
cioccolato m	cho·ko·*la*·to	chocolate
coda f	*ko*·da	tail • angler fish
conchiglie f pl	kon·*kee*·lye	pasta shells
condimento m	kon·dee·*men*·to	condiment • seasoning • dressing
contorni m pl	kon·*tor*·nee	side dishes • vegetables
costine f pl	kos·*tee*·ne	ribs
cozze f pl	*ko*·tse	mussels
crespella f	kres·*pe*·la	thin fritter
crostata f	kro·*sta*·ta	fruit tart • crust
crostini m pl	kro·*stee*·nee	slices of bread toasted with savoury toppings
crudo/a m/f	*kroo*·do/a	raw
della casa	de·la *ka*·za	'of the house' – house speciality
dolce m	*dol*·che	dessert • sweet
erbe f pl	*er*·be	herbs
fagiano m	fa·*ja*·no	pheasant

fagioli m pl	fa·*jo*·lee	beans
farcito/a m/f	far·*chee*·to/a	stuffed
farfalle f pl	far·*fa*·le	butterfly-shaped pasta
farinata f	fa·ree·*na*·ta	thin, flat bread made from chickpea flour
fetta f	*fe*·ta	a slice
fettuccine f pl	fe·too·*chee*·ne	long ribbon-shaped pasta
filetto m	fee·*le*·to	fillet
focaccia f	fo·*ka*·cha	flat bread often filled/topped with cheese, ham, vegetables & other ingredients
formaggio m	for·*ma*·jo	cheese
fragole f pl	*fra*·go·le	strawberries
fresco/a m/f	*fres*·ko/a	fresh
frittata f	free·*ta*·ta	thick omelette slice, served hot or cold
frittelle f pl	free·*te*·le	fritters
fritto/a m/f	*free*·to/a	fried
frumento m	froo·*men*·to	wheat
frutta f	*froo*·ta	fruit
frutti m pl *di mare*	*froo*·tee dee *ma*·re	sea food
funghi m pl	*foon*·gee	mushrooms
gambero m	*gam*·be·ro	prawn • shrimp
gamberoni m pl	gam·be·*ro*·nee	prawns
gelato m	je·*la*·to	ice cream
gnocchi m pl	*nyo*·kee	small dumplings – most commonly potato dumplings

gorgonzola f	gor·gon·*dzo*·la	spicy, sweet, creamy blue vein cow's milk cheese
granita f	gra·*nee*·ta	finely crushed flavoured ice
grappa f	*gra*·pa	distilled grape must
insalata f	een·sa·*la*·ta	salad
involtini m pl	een·vol·*tee*·nee	stuffed rolls of meat or fish
lenticchie f pl	len·*tee*·kye	lentils
lievito m	*lye*·vee·to	yeast
limone m	lee·*mo*·ne	lemon
lingua f	*leen*·gwa	tongue
linguine f pl	leen·*gwee*·ne	long thin ribbons of pasta
luganega f	loo·*ga*·ne·ga	pork sausage
lumache f pl	loo·*ma*·ke	snails
maccheroni m pl	ma·ke·*ro*·nee	any tube pasta
marinato/a m/f	ma·ree·*na*·to/a	marinated
mascarpone m	mas·kar·*po*·ne	very soft & creamy cheese
melanzane f pl	me·lan·*dza*·ne	eggplants • aubergines
minestra f	mee·*ne*·stra	general word for soup
minestrone m	mee·ne·*stro*·ne	traditional vegetable soup
misto/a m/f	*mees*·to/a	mixed
noce m	*no*·che	nut • walnut
non troppo cotto/a m/f	non *tro*·po *ko*·to/a	medium rare
olio m	*o*·lyo	oil — almost always olive oil
ossobuco m	o·so·*boo*·ko	veal shanks
ostriche f pl	*os*·tree·ke	oysters
pancetta f	pan·*che*·ta	salt-cured bacon
pane m	*pa*·ne	bread
panino m	pa·*nee*·no	bread roll

panzanella f	pan·tsa·*ne*·la	tomato, onion, garlic, olive oil, bread & basil salad
patate f pl	pa·*ta*·te	potatoes
pecorino m	pe·ko·*ree*·no	hard & spicy cheese
(*romano*)	(ro·*ma*·no)	made from ewe's milk
penne f pl	*pe*·ne	short & tubular pasta
peperoncini m pl	pe·pe·ron·*chee*·nee	hot chilli
peperoni m pl	pe·pe·*ro*·nee	peppers • capsicum
pesto m	*pes*·to	paste made from garlic, basil, pine nuts & Parmesan
poco cotto/a m/f	*po*·ko *ko*·to/a	rare
polenta f	po·*len*·ta	corn meal porridge
polpette m	pol·*pe*·te	meatballs
pomodori m pl	po·mo·*do*·ree	tomatoes
prosciutto m	pro·*shoo*·to	basic name for many types of thinly-sliced ham
quattro formaggi	*kwa*·tro for·*ma*·jee	pasta sauce with four different cheeses
quattro stagioni	*kwa*·tro sta·*jo*·nee	pizza with different toppings on each quarter
ragù m	ra·*goo*	generally a meat sauce but sometimes vegetarian
ravioli m pl	ra·vee·*o*·lee	pasta squares usually stuffed with meat, parmesan cheese & breadcrumbs
rigatoni m pl	ree·ga·*to*·nee	short, fat tubes of pasta
ripieno m	ree·*pye*·no	stuffing
riso m	*ree*·zo	rice

risotto m	ree-*zo*-to	rice dish slowly cooked in broth to a creamy consistency
rucola f	*roo*-ko-la	rocket
salsa f	*sal*-sa	sauce
salsiccia f	sal-*see*-cha	sausage
spaghetti m pl	spa-*ge*-tee	ubiquitous long thin strands of pasta
spalla f	*spa*-la	shoulder
speck m	spek	type of smoked ham
suppa f	*soo*-pa	soup
tacchino m	ta-*kee*-no	turkey
tagliatelle f	ta-lya-*te*-le	long, ribbon-shaped pasta
tartufo m	tar-*too*-fo	truffle (very expensive kind of mushroom)
tiramisù m	tee-ra-mee-*soo*	sponge cake soaked in coffee & arranged in layers with mascarpone, then sprinkled with cocoa
torta f	*tor*-ta	cake • tart • pie
tortellini m pl	tor-te-*lee*-nee	pasta filled with meat, parmesan & egg
uova m pl	*wo*-va	eggs
uva f pl	*oo*-va	grapes
verdure f pl	ver-*doo*-re	vegetables
vino m *della casa*	*vee*-no de-la *ka*-sa	house wine
vitello m	vee-*te*-lo	veal
vongole f pl	*von*-go-le	clams
zucca f	*tsoo*-ka	pumpkin
zucchero m	*tsoo*-ke-ro	sugar
zuppa f	*tsoo*-pa	soup

SERVICES
Post office

I want to send a ...	*Vorrei mandare un/una ...* m/f	vo·*ray* man·*da*·re oon/*oo*·na ...
fax	*fax* m	faks
letter	*lettera* f	*le*·te·ra
parcel	*pacchetto* m	pa·*ke*·to
postcard	*cartolina* f	kar·to·*lee*·na

I want to buy ...	*Vorrei comprare ...*	vo·*ray* kom·*pra*·re ...
an aerogram	*un aerogramma*	oo·na·e·ro·*gra*·ma
an envelope	*una busta*	*oo*·na *boo*·sta
stamps	*dei francobolli*	day fran·ko·*bo*·lee

Please send it (to Australia) by ...	*Lo mandi ... (in Australia), per favore.*	lo *man*·dee ... (ee·now·*stra*·lya) per fa·*vo*·re
airmail	*via aerea*	*vee*·a a·e·re·a
express mail	*posta prioritaria*	*pos*·ta pryo·ree·*ta*·rya
regular mail	*posta ordinaria*	*pos*·ta or·dee·*na*·rya
sea mail	*via* f *mare*	*vee*·a *ma*·re

Bank

Where's the nearest ...?	*Dov'è ... più vicino?*	do·*ve* ... pyoo vee·*chee*·no
automatic teller machine	*il Bancomat*	eel *ban*·ko·mat
foreign exchange office	*il cambio*	eel *kam*·byo

49

I'd like to ...	Vorrei ...	vo·ray ...
Where can I ...?	Dove posso ...?	do·ve po·so ...
arrange a transfer	trasferire	tras·fe·ree·re
	soldi	sol·dee
cash a cheque	riscuotere	ree·skwo·te·re
	un assegno	oo·na·se·nyo
change money	cambiare denaro	kam·bya·re de·na·ro
change a travellers cheque	cambiare un assegno	kam·bya·re oo·na·se·nyo
	di viaggio	dee vee·a·jo
get a cash advance	prelevare con carta di credito	pre·le·va·re kon kar·ta dee kre·dee·to
withdraw money	fare un prelievo	fa·re oon pre·lye·vo

What's the ...?	Quant'è ...?	kwan·te ...
commission	la commissione	la ko·mee·syo·ne
exchange rate	il cambio	eel kam·byo

What's the charge for that?
Quanto costa? — kwan·to kos·ta

What time does the bank open?
A che ora apre la banca? — a ke o·ra a·pre la ban·ka

Phone

What's your phone number?
Qual'è il Suo/tuo numero di telefono? pol/inf — kwa·le eel soo·o/too·o noo·me·ro dee te·le·fo·no

Where's the nearest public phone?
Dov'è il telefono pubblico più vicino? — do·ve eel te·le·fo·no poo·blee·ko pyoo vee·chee·no

I want to make a ...	*Vorrei fare ...*	vo·*ray fa*·re ...
call	*una chiamata*	*oo*·na kya·*ma*·ta
local call	*una chiamata*	*oo*·na kya·*ma*·ta
	locale	lo·*ka*·le
reverse-charge/	*una chiamata a*	*oo*·na kya·*ma*·ta a
collect call	*carico del*	*ka*·ree·ko del
	destinatario	des·tee·na·*ta*·ryo
How much	*Quanto costa ...?*	kwan·to *kos*·ta ...
does ... cost?		
a (three)-minute	*una telefonata*	*oo*·na te·le·fo·*na*·ta
call	*di (tre) minuti*	dee (tre) mee·*noo*·tee
each extra	*ogni minuto*	*o*·nyee mee·*noo*·to
minute	*in più*	een pyoo

I'd like to buy a phonecard.
Vorrei comprare una   vo·*ray* kom·*pra*·re *oo*·na
scheda telefonica.   *ske*·da te·le·*fo*·nee·ka

The number is ...
Il numero è ...   eel *noo*·me·ro e ...

Can I speak to ...?
Posso parlare con ...?   *po*·so par·*la*·re kon ...

Please tell him/her I called.
Gli/Le dica che ho   lyee/le *dee*·ka ke o
telefonato, per favore.   te·le·fo·*na*·to per fa·*vo*·re

Mobile/cell phone

What are the rates?
Quali sono le tariffe?   kwa·lee *so*·no le ta·*ree*·fe

(30c) per (30) seconds.
(Trenta centesimi)   (*tren*·ta chen·*te*·zee·mee)
per (trenta) secondi.   per (*tren*·ta) se·*kon*·dee

I'd like a/an ...	Vorrei ...	vo·ray ...
adaptor plug	un adattatore	oo·na·da·ta·to·re
charger for my phone	un carica-batterie	oon ka·ree·ka·ba·te·ree·e
mobile phone/ cellphone for hire	un cellulare da noleggiare	oon che·loo·la·re da no·le·ja·re
prepaid mobile phone/cellphone	un cellulare prepagato	oon che·loo·la·re pre·pa·ga·to
SIM card for your network	un SIM card per la rete telefonica	oon seem kard per la re·te te·le·fo·nee·ka

Internet

Where's the local Internet café?
Dove si trova l'Internet point? — do·ve see tro·va leen·ter·net poynt

How much per hour?
Quanto costa all'ora? — kwan·to kos·ta a·lo·ra

How much per page?
Quanto costa a pagina? — kwan·to kos·ta a pa·jee·na

Can you help me change to English-language preference?
Mi può aiutare a cambiare la lingua in inglese — mee pwo ai·yoo·ta·re a kam·bya·re la leen·gwa een een·gle·ze

It's crashed.
Si è bloccato. — see e blo·ka·to

I'd like to ...	Vorrei ...	vo·ray ...
check my email	controllare le mie email	kon·tro·la·re le mee·e e·mayl
get Internet access	usare Internet	oo·za·re een·ter·net
use a printer	usare una stampante	oo·za·re oo·na stam·pan·te

GO
Directions

Where's the ...?	Dov'è ...?	do·ve ...
bank	la banca	la ban·ka
hotel	l'albergo	lal·ber·go
police station	il posto di polizia	eel pos·to dee po·lee·tsee·a

Can you show me (on the map)?
Può mostrarmi (sulla pianta)?   pwo mos·trar·mee (soo·la pyan·ta)

What's the address?
Qual'è l'indirizzo?   kwa·le leen·dee·ree·tso

How do I get there?
Come ci si arriva?   ko·me chee see a·ree·va

How far is it?
Quant'è distante?   kwan·te dees·tan·te

It's ...	È ...	e ...
behind ...	dietro ...	dye·tro ...
far away	lontano	lon·ta·no
here	qui	kwee
in front of ...	davanti a ...	da·van·tee a ...
left	a sinistra	a see·nee·stra
near (to ...)	vicino (a ...)	vee·chee·no (a ...)
next to ...	accanto a ...	a·kan·to a ...
on the corner	all'angolo	a lan·go·lo
opposite ...	di fronte a ...	dee fron·te a ...
right	a destra	a de·stra
straight ahead	sempre diritto	sem·pre dee·ree·to
there	là	la

It's ...	È a ...	e a ...
(100) metres	(cento) metri	(chen·to) me·tree
(10) minutes	(dieci) minuti	(dye·chee) mee·noo·tee

Turn ...	Giri ...	jee·ree ...
at the corner	all'angolo	a·lan·go·lo
at the traffic lights	al semaforo	al se·ma·fo·ro
left	a sinistra	a see·nee·stra
right	a destra	a de·stra

by bus	con l'autobus	kon low·to·boos
on foot	a piedi	a pye·dee
by metro	con la metropolitana	kon la me·tro·po·lee·ta·na
by taxi	con il tassì	ko·neel ta·see
by train	con il treno	ko·neel tre·no

north	al nord	al nord
south	al sud	al sood
east	all'est	al·est
west	all'ovest	al·o·vest

Getting around

What time does the ... leave?	A che ora parte ...?	a ke o·ra par·te ...
boat	la nave	la na·ve
bus	l'autobus	low·to·boos
metro	la metropolitana	la me·tro·po·lee·ta·na
plane	l'aereo	la·e·re·o
train	il treno	eel tre·no

What time's	A che ora passa	a ke *o*·ra *pa*·sa
the ... bus?	... autobus	... *ow*·to·boos
first	il primo	eel *pree*·mo
last	l'ultimo	*lool*·tee·mo
next	il prossimo	eel *pro*·see·mo

How many stops to ...?
Quante fermate mancano ...? kwan·te fer·*ma*·te man·ka·no ...

Is this seat free?
È libero questo posto? e *lee*·be·ro kwe·sto *pos*·to

That's my seat.
Quel posto è mio. kwel *pos*·to e *mee*·o

Can you tell me when we get to ...?
Mi sa dire quando mee sa *dee*·re kwan·do
arriviamo a ...? a·ree·*vya*·mo a ...

I want to get off ...	Voglio scendere ...	*vo*·lyo shen·de·re ...
at the Colosseum	al Colosseo	al ko·lo·*se*·o
here	qui	kwee

Tickets & luggage

Where can I buy a ticket?
Dove posso comprare un *do*·ve *po*·so kom·*pra*·re oon
biglietto? bee·*lye*·to

Do I need to book (a seat)?
Bisogna prenotare bee·*zo*·nya pre·no·*ta*·re
(un posto)? (oon *pos*·to)

How long does the trip take?
Quanto ci vuole? *kwan*·to chee *vwo*·le

I'd like to ... my ticket, please.	Vorrei ... il mio biglietto, per favore.	vo·*ray* ... eel *mee*·o bee·*lye*·to per fa·*vo*·re
cancel	cancellare	kan·che·*la*·re
change	cambiare	kam·*bya*·re
collect	ritirare	ree·tee·*ra*·re
confirm	confermare	kon·fer·*ma*·re

How much is it?	Quant'è?	kwan·*te*

One ... ticket (to Rome), please.	Un biglietto ... (per Roma), per favore.	oon bee·*lye*·to ... (per *ro*·ma) per fa·*vo*·re
1st-class	di prima classe	dee *pree*·ma *kla*·se
2nd-class	di seconda classe	dee se·*kon*·da *kla*·se
child's	per bambini	per bam·*bee*·nee
one-way	di sola andata	dee *so*·la an·*da*·ta
return	di andata e ritorno	dee an·*da*·ta e ree·*tor*·no
student's	per studenti	per stoo·*den*·tee

I'd like a/an ... seat, please.	Vorrei un posto ..., per favore.	vo·*ray* oon *pos*·to ... per fa·*vo*·re
aisle	sul corridoio	sool ko·ree·*do*·yo
nonsmoking	per non fumatori	per non foo·ma·*to*·ree
smoking	per fumatori	per foo·ma·*to*·ree
window	vicino al finestrino	vee·*chee*·no al fee·nes·*tree*·no

Is there air-conditioning?
C'è l'aria condizionata?   che *la*·rya kon·dee·tsyo·*na*·ta

Is there a toilet?
C'è un gabinetto?   che oon ga·bee·*ne*·to

GO

Is it a direct route?
    È un itinerario diretto?   e oo·nee·tee·ne·*ra*·ryo dee·*re*·to

What time do I have to check in?
    A che ora devo presentarmi   a ke o·ra *de*·vo pre·zen·*tar*·mee
    per l'accettazione?   per la·che·ta·*tsyo*·ne

Can I get a stand-by ticket?
    Posso mettermi in   *po*·so *me*·ter·mee een
    lista d'attesa?   *lees*·ta da·*te*·za

Where's the baggage claim?
    Dov'è il ritiro bagagli?   do·*ve* eel ree·*tee*·ro ba·*ga*·lyee

I'd like a luggage locker.
    Vorrei un armadietto   vo·*ray* oo·nar·ma·*dye*·to
    per il bagaglio.   per eel ba·*ga*·lyo

Can I have some coins/tokens?
    Può darmi della moneta/   pwo *dar*·mee *de*·la mo·*ne*·ta/
    dei gettoni?   day je·*to*·nee

My luggage	*Il mio bagaglio*	eel *mee*·o ba·*ga*·lyo
has been …	*è stato …*	e *sta*·to …
damaged	*danneggiato*	da·ne·*ja*·to
lost	*perso*	*per*·so
stolen	*rubato*	roo·*ba*·to

Bus, metro, taxi & train

Which bus goes to …?
    Quale autobus va a …?   *kwa*·le *ow*·to·boos va a …

Is this the bus to …?
    Questo autobus va a …?   *kwe*·sto *ow*·to·boos va a …

What station is this?
    Che stazione è questa?   ke sta·*tsyo*·ne e *kwe*·sta

What's the next station?
Qual'è la prossima stazione?   kwa·*le* la *pro*·see·ma sta·*tsyo*·ne

Does this train stop at (Milan)?
Questo treno si ferma a (Milano)?   *kwe*·sto *tre*·no see *fer*·ma a (mee·*la*·no)

Do I need to change trains?
Devo cambiare treno?   *de*·vo kam·*bya*·re *tre*·no

Which carriage is for (Rome)?
Quale carrozza è per (Roma)?   kwa·le ka·*ro*·tsa e per (*ro*·ma)

Which carriage is (1st class)?
Quale carrozza è (di prima classe?)   kwa·le ka·*ro*·tsa e (dee *pree*·ma *kla*·se)

Where's the dining car?
Dov'è il vagone ristorante?   do·*ve* eel va·*go*·ne rees·to·*ran*·te

Where's the taxi stand?
Dov'è la fermata dei tassì?   do·*ve* la fer·*ma*·ta day ta·*see*

I'd like a taxi ...	*Vorrei un tassì ...*	vo·*ray* oon ta·*see* ...
at (9am)	*alle (nove di mattina)*	*a*·le (*no*·ve dee ma·*tee*·na)
now	*adesso*	a·*de*·so
tomorrow	*domani*	do·*ma*·nee

Is this taxi free?
È libero questo tassì?   e *lee*·be·ro *kwe*·sto ta·*see*

How much is it to ...?
Quant'è per ...?   kwan·*te* per ...

Please put the meter on.
Usi il tassametro, per favore.   *oo*·zee eel ta·sa·*me*·tro per fa·*vo*·re

GO

Please take me to (this address).

Mi porti a (questo indirizzo), per piacere. mee *por*·tee a (*kwe*·sto een·dee·*ree*·tso) per pya·*che*·re

Please ...	*..., per favore.*	... per fa·*vo*·re
slow down	*Rallenti*	ra·*len*·tee
wait here	*Mi aspetti qui*	mee as·*pe*·tee kwee

Stop ...	*Si fermi ...*	see *fer*·mee ...
at the corner	*all'angolo*	a *lan*·go·lo
here	*qui*	kwee

Car & motorbike hire

I'd like to hire a ...	*Vorrei noleggiare ...*	vo·*ray* no·le·*ja*·re ...
(large/small) car	*una macchina (grande/piccola)*	*oo*·na ma·*kee*·na (*gran*·de/*pee*·ko·la)
motorbike	*una moto*	*oo*·na *mo*·to

with/without ...	*con/senza ...*	kon/*sen*·tsa ...
air-conditioning	*aria condizionata*	*a*·rya kon·dee·tsyo·*na*·ta
antifreeze	*anticongelante*	an·tee·kon·je·*lan*·te
snow chains	*le catene da neve*	le ka·*te*·ne da *ne*·ve

How much for ... hire?	*Quanto costa ...?*	*kwan*·to *kos*·ta ...
daily	*al giorno*	al *jor*·no
hourly	*all'ora*	a·*lo*·ra
weekly	*alla settimana*	*a*·la se·tee·*ma*·na

Does that include …?	*È compreso/a … m/f*	e kom·*pre*·zo/a …
mileage	*il chilometraggio* m	eel kee·lo·me·*tra*·jo
insurance	*l'assicurazione* f	la·see·koo·ra·*tsyo*·ne

What's the speed limit?
Qual'è il limite di   kwa·*le* eel *lee*·mee·te dee
velocità?   ve·lo·chee·*ta*

Is this the road to …?
Questa strada porta a …?   *kwe*·sta *stra*·da *por*·ta a …

Where's a service station?
Dov'è una stazione   do·*ve* oo·na sta·*tsyo*·ne
di servizio?   dee ser·*vee*·tsyo

(How long) Can I park here?
(Per quanto tempo) Posso   (per kwan·to tem·po) *po*·so
parcheggiare qui?   par·ke·*ja*·re kwee

leaded	*benzina* f *con piombo*	ben·*dzee*·na kon *pyom*·bo
unleaded	*benzina* f *senza piombo*	ben·*dzee*·na *sen*·tsa *pyom*·bo

Road signs

Dare la Precedenza	*da*·re la pre·che·*den*·tsa	Give Way
Divieto di Accesso	dee·*vye*·to dee a·*che*·so	No Entry
Entrata	en·*tra*·ta	Entrance
Pedaggio	pe·*da*·jo	Toll
Senso Unico	*sen*·so *oo*·nee·ko	One Way
Stop	stop	Stop
Uscita	oo·*shee*·ta	Exit

GO

SLEEP
Finding accommodation

Where's a/an ...?	Dov'è ...?	do·ve ...
bed & breakfast	un bed e breakfast	oon bed e brek·fast
camping ground	un campeggio	oon kam·pe·jo
guesthouse	una pensione	oo·na pen·syo·ne
hotel	un albergo	oo·nal·ber·go
inn (budget hotel)	una locanda	oo·na lo·kan·da
room	una camera	oo·na ka·me·ra
youth hostel	un ostello della gioventù	oo·nos·te·lo de·la jo·ven·too

Can you recommend somewhere ...?	Può consigliare qualche posto ...?	pwo kon·see·lya·re kwal·ke pos·to ...
cheap	economico	e·ko·no·mee·ko
good	buono	bwo·no
luxurious	di lusso	dee loo·so
nearby	vicino	vee·chee·no
romantic	romantico	ro·man·tee·ko

What's the address?
Qual'è l'indirizzo? kwa·le leen·dee·ree·tso

How do I get there?
Come ci si arriva? ko·me chee see a·ree·va

For responses, see **GO**, page 53.

SLEEP

Booking ahead & checking in

I'd like to book a room, please.

Vorrei prenotare una camera,
per favore.

vo·*ray* pre·no·*ta*·re *oo*·na *ka*·me·ra
per fa·*vo*·re

I have a reservation.

Ho una prenotazione.

o *oo*·na pre·no·ta·*tsyo*·ne

My name's ...

Mi chiamo ...

mee *kya*·mo ...

Do you have a	*Avete una*	a·*ve*·te *oo*·na
... room?	*camera ...?*	*ka*·me·ra ...
double	*doppia con letto*	do·*pya* kon le·*to*
	matrimoniale	ma·tree·mo·*nya*·le
single	*singola*	*seen*·go·la
twin	*doppia a*	do·pya a
	due letti	*doo*·e le·tee

How much is it	*Quanto costa*	*kwan*·to *kos*·ta
per ...?	*per ...?*	per ...
night	*una notte*	*oo*·na *no*·te
person	*persona*	per·*so*·na
week	*una settimana*	*oo*·na se·tee·*ma*·na

I'd like to stay for (two) nights.

Vorrei rimanere
(due) notti.

vo·*ray* ree·ma·*ne*·re
(*doo*·e) *no*·tee

From (July 2) to (July 6).

Dal (due luglio) al (sei luglio).   dal (*doo*·e *loo*·lyo) al (say *loo*·lyo)

There are (three) of us.

Siamo (tre).

sya·mo (tre)

SLEEP

62

Can I see it?
Posso vederla? po·so ve·*der*·la

It's fine. I'll take it.
Va bene. La prendo. va *be*·ne la *pren*·do

Do I need to pay upfront?
Devo pagare in anticipo? *de*·vo pa·*ga*·re ee·nan·*tee*·chee·po

Can I pay ...? *Posso pagare con ...?* po·so pa·*ga*·re kon ...
  by credit card   *la carta di* la *kar*·ta dee
    credito kre·dee·to
  with a travellers *un assegno di* oo·na·*se*·nyo dee
  cheque   *viaggio* vee·*a*·jo

For methods of payment, see also **PAYING**, page 29 and **BANK**, page 49.

Requests & queries

When's breakfast served?
A che ora è la prima colazione? a ke *o*·ra e la *pree*·ma ko·la·*tsyo*·ne

Where's breakfast served?
Dove si prende la *do*·ve see *pren*·de la
prima colazione? *pree*·ma ko·la·*tsyo*·ne

Please wake me at (seven).
Mi svegli (alle sette), per favore. mee *sve*·lyee (a·le *se*·te) per fa·*vo*·re

Could I have my key, please?
Può darmi la mia chiave, pwo *dar*·mee la *mee*·a *kya*·ve
per favore? per fa·*vo*·re

Could I have a receipt, please?
Può darmi una ricevuta, pwo *dar*·mee oo·na ree·che·*voo*·ta
per favore? per fa·*vo*·re

Can I use the ...?	Posso usare ...?	po·so oo·za·re ...
kitchen	la cucina	la koo·chee·na
laundry	la lavanderia	la la·van·de·ree·a
telephone	il telefono	eel te·le·fo·no

Do you have a/an ...?	C'è ...?	che ...
elevator	un ascensore	oo·na·shen·so·re
laundry service	il servizio	eel ser·vee·tsyo
	lavanderia	la·van·de·ree·a
safe	una cassaforte	oo·na ka·sa·for·te
swimming pool	una piscina	oo·na pee·shee·na

Do you arrange tours here?
Si organizzano le gite qui? see or·ga·nee·dza·no le jee·te kwee

Do you change money here?
Si cambiano i soldi qui? see kam·bya·no ee sol·dee kwee

The room is too ...	La camera è troppo ...	la ka·me·ra e tro·po ...
cold	fredda	fre·da
dark	scura	skoo·ra
expensive	cara	ka·ra
light/bright	luminosa	loo·mee·no·za
noisy	rumorosa	roo·mo·ro·za
small	piccola	pee·ko·la

The ... doesn't work.	... non funziona.	... non foon·tsyo·na
air-conditioning	L'aria	la·rya
	condizionata	kon·dee·tsyo·na·ta
fan	Il ventilatore	eel ven·tee·la·to·re
toilet	Il gabinetto	eel ga·bee·ne·to
window	La finestra	la fee·nes·tra

Can I get another ...?	Può darmi un altro/a ... m/f	pwo *dar*·mee oo·*nal*·tro/a
This ... isn't clean.	Questo/a ... non è pulito/a. m/f	*kwe*·sto/a ... non e poo·*lee*·to/a
blanket	coperta f	ko·*per*·ta
pillow	cuscino m	koo·*shee*·no
pillowcase	federa f	*fe*·de·ra
towel	asciugamano m	a·shoo·ga·*ma*·no

Checking out

What time is checkout?

| A che ora si deve lasciar libera la camera? | a ke o·*ra* see *de*·ve la·*shar* *lee*·be·ra la *ka*·me·ra |

Can I leave my luggage here until ....?	Posso lasciare il mio bagaglio qui fino ...?	*po*·so la·*sha*·re eel *mee*·o ba·*ga*·lyo kwee *fee*·no ...
next week	alla settimana prossima	a·la se·tee·*ma*·na pro·*see*·ma
tonight	a stasera	a sta·*se*·ra
Wednesday	a mercoledì	a mer·ko·le·*dee*

Could I have my ...., please?	Posso avere ..., per favore?	*po*·so a·*ve*·re ... per fa·*vo*·re
deposit	la caparra	la ka·*pa*·ra
passport	il mio passaporto	eel *mee*·o pa·sa·*por*·to
valuables	i miei oggetti di valore	ee myay o·*je*·tee dee va·*lo*·re

I'll be back ...	Torno ...	*tor*·no ...
in (three) days	fra (tre) giorni	fra (tre) *jor*·nee
on (Tuesday)	(martedì)	(mar·te·*dee*)

WORK
Introductions

I'm attending a ...?	*Sono qui per un/una ...* m/f	*so*·no kwee per oon/*oo*·na ...
Where's the ...?	*Dov'è il/la ...?* m/f	do·*ve* eel/la ...
business centre	*business centre* m	*beez*·nees *sen*·ter
conference	*conferenza* f	kon·fe·*ren*·tsa
course	*corso* m	*kor*·so
meeting	*riunione* f	ree·oo·*nyo*·ne
trade fair	*fiera* f *commerciale*	*fye*·ra ko·mer·*cha*·le
I'm here with ...	*Sono qui con ...*	*so*·no kwee kon ...
(the UN)	*(l'ONU)*	(lo·*noo*)
my colleagues	*i miei colleghi*	ee myay ko·*le*·gee
(two) others	*(due) altri*	(*doo*·e) *al*·tree

Here's my business card.
Ecco il mio biglietto da visita.
e·ko eel *mee*·o bee·*lye*·to da *vee*·zee·ta

Let me introduce my colleague.
Vorrei presentare il mio collega. m
vo·*ray* pre·sen·*ta*·re eel *mee*·o ko·*le*·ga
Vorrei presentare la mia collega. f
vo·*ray* pre·sen·*ta*·re la *mee*·a ko·*le*·ga

I'm alone.
Sono solo/a. m/f
so·no *so*·lo/a

I'm here for (two) days/weeks.
Sono qui per (due) giorni/ settimane.
so·no kwee per (*doo*·e) jor·nee/ se·tee·*ma*·ne

I'm staying at ..., room ...
Alloggio al ..., camera ...
a·*lo*·jo al ..., *ka*·me·ra ...

Business needs

I have an appointment with ...
Ho un appuntamento con ...   o oo·na·poon·ta·*men*·to kon ...

I need an interpreter.
Ho bisogno di un interprete.   o bee·*zo*·nyo dee oo·neen·*ter*·pre·te

I'm expecting a ...	*Aspetto ...*	a·*spet*·o ...
call	*una telefonata*	*oo*·na te·le·fo·*na*·ta
fax	*un fax*	oon faks

I need ...	*Ho bisogno di ...*	o bee·*zon*·yo dee ...
to use a	*usare un*	oo·*sa*·re oon
computer	*computer*	kom·*pyoo*·ter
to send an	*mandare un*	man·*da*·re oon
email/fax	*email/fax*	e·*mayl*/faks

Is there a/an ...?	*C'è ...?*	che ...
data projector	*un proiettore*	oon pro·ye·*to*·re
laser pointer	*una penna ottica*	*oo*·na *pe*·na o·*tee*·ka
overhead	*una lavagna*	*oo*·na la·*va*·nya
projector	*luminosa*	loo·mee·*no*·sa

After the deal

That went very well.
È andato bene.   e an·*da*·to *be*·ne

Shall we go for a drink/meal?
Andiamo a bere/   an·*dya*·mo a *be*·re/
mangiare qualcosa?   man·*ja*·re kwal·*ko*·za

It's on me.
Offro io.   o·fro ee·o

For additional terms, see **SERVICES**, page 49.

HELP
Emergencies

Help!	Aiuto!	ai·yoo·to
Stop!	Fermi!	fer·mee
Go away!	Vai via!	vai vee·a
Thief!	Ladro!	la·dro
Fire!	Al fuoco!	al fwo·ko
Watch out!	Attenzione!	a·ten·tsyo·ne
Call ...	Chiami ...	kya·mee ...
an ambulance	un'ambulanza	o·nam·boo·lan·tsa
a doctor	un medico	oon me·dee·ko
the fire brigade	i vigili del fuoco	ee vee·jee·lee del fwo·ko
the police	la polizia	la po·lee·tsee·a

It's an emergency!
È un'emergenza! e oo·ne·mer·jen·tsa

Could you help me, please?
Mi può aiutare, per favore? mee pwo ai·yoo·ta·re per fa·vo·re

I have to use the telephone.
Devo fare una telefonata. de·vo fa·re oo·na te·le·fo·na·ta

I'm lost.
Mi sono perso/a. m/f mee so·no per·so/a

Where are the toilets?
Dove sono i gabinetti? do·ve so·no ee ga·bee·ne·tee

Leave me alone!
Lasciami in pace! la·sha·mee een pa·che

Police

Where's the police station?
Dov'è il posto di polizia?   do·*ve* eel *pos*·to dee po·lee·*tsee*·a

I want to report an offence.
Voglio fare una denuncia.   vo·lyo *fa*·re *oo*·na de·*noon*·cha

I've been raped.
Sono stato/a violentato/a. m/f   so·no *sta*·to/a vyo·len·*ta*·to/a

I've been assaulted.
Sono stato aggredito/a. m/f   so·no *sta*·to/a a·gre·*dee*·to/a

I've been robbed.
Sono stato/a derubato/a. m/f   so·no *sta*·to/a de·roo·*ba*·to/a

I've lost my ... My ... was/were stolen.	*Ho perso ...* *Mi hanno* *rubato ...*	o *per*·so ... mee *a*·no roo·*ba*·to ...
backpack	*il mio zaino*	eel *mee*·o *dzai*·no
bags	*i miei* *bagagli*	ee mee·*ay* ba·*ga*·lyee
credit card	*la mia carta* *di credito*	la *mee*·a *kar*·ta dee *kre*·dee·to
handbag	*la mia borsa*	la *mee*·a *bor*·sa
jewellery	*i miei gioielli*	ee mee·*ay* jo·*ye*·lee
money	*i miei soldi*	ee mee·*ay* *sol*·dee
passport	*il mio* *passaporte*	eel *mee*·o pa·sa·*por*·te
travellers cheques	*i miei* *assegni di* *viaggio*	ee mee·*ay* a·*se*·nyee dee vee·*a*·jo
wallet	*portafoglio*	por·ta·*fo*·lyo

I want to	Vorrei	vo·*ray*
contact my ...	contattare ...	kon·ta·*ta*·re ...
embassy	*la mia ambasciata*	la *mee*·a am·ba·*sha*·ta
consulate	*il mio consolato*	eel *mee*·o kon·so·*la*·to

I have insurance.
Ho l'assicurazione.   o la·see·koo·ra·*tsyo*·ne

Can I have a receipt for my insurance?
Può darmi una ricevuta per   pwo *dar*·mee *oo*·na ree·che·*voo*·ta per
la mia assicurazione?   la *mee*·a a·see·koo·ra·*tsyo*·ne

I have a prescription for this drug.
Ho una ricetta per questa   o *oo*·na re·*che*·ta per *kwe*·sta
medicina.   me·dee·*chee*·na

Health

Where's the	Dov'è ... più	do·*ve* ... pyoo
nearest ...?	*vicino/a?* m/f	vee·*chee*·no/a
(night) chemist	*la farmacia* f	la far·ma·*chee*·a
	(di turno)	(dee *toor*·no)
dentist	*il/la dentista* m/f	eel/la den·*tee*·sta
doctor	*il medico* m	eel *me*·dee·ko
hospital	*l'ospedale* m	los·pe·*da*·le
medical centre	*l'ambulatorio* m	lam·boo·la·*to*·ryo
optometrist	*l'ottico* m	*lo*·tee·ko

I need a doctor (who speaks English).
Ho bisogno di un medico   o bee·*zo*·nyo dee oon *me*·dee·ko
(che parli inglese).   (ke *par*·lee een·*gle*·ze)

Could I see a female doctor?
Posso vedere una dottoressa?   *po*·so ve·*de*·re *oo*·na do·to·*re*·sa

Can the doctor come here?
Può venire qui il medico?   pwo ve·*nee*·re kwee eel *me*·dee·ko

I've run out of my medication.
Ho finito la mia   o fee·*nee*·to la *mee*·a
medicina.   me·dee·*chee*·na

I've been	*Sono stato/a*	*so*·no *sta*·to/a
vaccinated for ...	*vaccinato/a per ...* m/f	va·chee·*na*·to/a per ...
hepatitis A/B/C	*l'epatite A/B/C*	le·pa·*tee*·te a/bee/chee
tetanus	*il tetano*	eel *te*·ta·no
typhoid	*il tifo*	eel *tee*·fo

I need ...	*Ho bisogno di ...*	o bee·*zo*·nyo dee ...
new glasses	*nuovi occhiali*	*nwo*·vee o·*kya*·lee
contact	*nuove lenti a*	*nwo*·ve *len*·tee a
lenses	*contatto*	kon·*ta*·to

Symptoms, conditions & allergies

I'm sick.
Mi sento male.   mee *sen*·to *ma*·le

I've been injured.
Sono stato/a ferito/a. m/f   *so*·no *sta*·to/a fe·*ree*·to/a

It hurts here.
Mi fa male qui.   mee fa *ma*·le kwee

I've been vomiting.
Ho vomitato alcune volte.   o vo·mee·*ta*·to al·*koo*·ne *vol*·te

I can't sleep.
Non riesco a dormire.   non *ryes*·ko a dor·*mee*·re

I feel ...	Mi sento ...	mee sen·to ...
better	meglio	me·lyo
strange	strano/a m/f	stra·no/a
weak	debole	de·bo·le
worse	peggio	pe·jo

I feel ...	Sono ...	so·no ...
anxious	ansioso/a m/f	an·syo·zo/a
depressed	depresso/a m/f	de·pre·so/a

I feel ...	Ho ...	o ...
dizzy	il capogiro	eel ka·po·gee·ro
hot and	vampate di	vam·pa·te dee
cold	calore	ka·lo·re
nauseous	la nausea	la now·ze·a
shivery	i brividi	ee bree·vee·dee

I have a/ an ...	Ho ...	o ...
allergy	un'allergia	oo·na·ler·jee·a
cold	un raffreddore	oon ra·fre·do·re
cough	la tosse	la to·se
diarrhoea	la diarrea	la dee·a·re·a
fever	la febbre	la fe·bre
headache	mal di testa	mal dee tes·ta
heart	un problema	oon pro·ble·ma
condition	cardiaco	kar·dya·ko
migraine	un'emicrania	oo·ne·mee·kran·ya
swelling	un gonfiore	oon gon·fyo·re
sore throat	mal di gola	mal dee go·la

I'm ...	Sono ...	so·no ...
asthmatic	asmatico/a m/f	az·ma·tee·ko/a
diabetic	diabetico/a m/f	dee·a·be·tee·ko/a
epileptic	epilettico/a m/f	e·pee·le·tee·ko/a

I've (recently) had ...

Ho avuto ...	o a·*voo*·to ...	
(di recente).	(dee re·*chen*·te)	

I'm on medication for ...

Prendo la   *pren*·do la

medicina per ...   me·dee·*chee*·na per ...

I need something for ...

Ho bisogno di   o bee·*zo*·nyo dee

qualcosa per ...   kwal·*ko*·za per ...

Do I need a prescription for ...?

C'è bisogno di una   che bee·*zo*·nyo dee *oo*·na

ricetta per ...?   re·*che*·ta per ...

How many times a day?

Quante volte al giorno?   *kwan*·te *vol*·te al *jor*·no

I'm allergic to ...   Sono   *so*·no

      allergico/a ... m/f   a·*ler*·jee·ko/a ...

antibiotics	agli anti-biotici	*a*·lyee an·tee-bee·o·tee·chee
anti-inflammatories	agli antinfiammatori	*a*·lyee an·teen·fya·ma·*to*·ree
aspirin	all'aspirina	a·las·pee·*ree*·na
bees	alle api	*a*·le *a*·pee
codeine	alla codeina	*a*·la ko·de·*ee*·na
penicillin	alla penicillina	*a*·la pe·nee·chee·*lee*·na
pollen	al polline	al po·*lee*·ne

I have a skin allergy.

Ho un'allergia alla pelle.   o oo·na·ler·*jee*·a *a*·la *pe*·le

For food-related allergies, see **EAT & DRINK**, page 41.

HELP

Numbers

0	zero	dze·ro		18	diciotto	dee·cho·to
1	uno	oo·no		19	diciannove	dee·cha·no·ve
2	due	doo·e		20	venti	ven·tee
3	tre	tre		21	ventuno	ven·too·no
4	quattro	kwa·tro		22	ventidue	ven·tee·doo·e
5	cinque	cheen·kwe		30	trenta	tren·ta
6	sei	say		40	quaranta	kwa·ran·ta
7	sette	se·te		50	cinquanta	cheen·kwan·ta
8	otto	o·to		60	sessanta	se·san·ta
9	nove	no·ve		70	settanta	se·tan·ta
10	dieci	dye·chee		80	ottanta	o·tan·ta
11	undici	oon·dee·chee		90	novanta	no·van·ta
12	dodici	do·dee·chee		91	novantuno	no·van·too·no
13	tredici	tre·dee·chee		100	cento	chen·to
14	quattordici	kwa·tor·dee·chee		200	duecento	doo·e·chen·to
15	quindici	kween·dee·chee		300	trecento	tre·chen·to
16	sedici	se·dee·chee		1,000	mille	mee·le
17	diciassette	dee·cha·se·te		2,000	duemila	doo·e·mee·la

Colours

dark ...

    ... *scuro/a* m/f   skoo·ro/a

light ...

    ... *chiaro/a* m/f   kya·ro/a

black	nero/a m/f	ne·ro/a		**pink**	rosa	ro·za
blue	azzurro/a m/f	a·dzoo·ro/a		**purple**	viola	vyo·la
brown	marrone	ma·ro·ne		**red**	rosso/a m/f	ro·so/a
green	verde	ver·de		**yellow**	giallo/a m/f	ja·lo/a
orange	arancione	a·ran·chyo·ne		**white**	bianco/a m/f	byan·ko/a

Time & dates

What time is it?	*Che ora è?*	ke *o*·ra e
It's one o'clock.	*È l'una.*	e *loo*·na
It's (two) o'clock.	*Sono le (due).*	*so*·no le (*doo*·e)
Five past (one).	*(L'una) e cinque.*	(*loo*·na) e *cheen*·kwe
Quarter past (one).	*(L'una) e un quarto.*	(*loo*·na) e oon *kwar*·to
Half past (one).	*(L'una) e mezza.*	(*loo*·na) e *me*·dza
Quarter to (eight).	*(Le otto) meno un quarto.*	(le *o*·to) *me*·no oon *kwar*·to
Twenty to (eight).	*(Le otto) meno venti.*	(le *o*·to) *me*·no *ven*·tee
At what time ...?	*A che ora ...?*	a ke *o*·ra ...
At ...	*Alle ...*	*a*·le ...

Monday	*lunedì*	loo·ne·*dee*
Tuesday	*martedì*	mar·te·*dee*
Wednesday	*mercoledì*	mer·ko·le·*dee*
Thursday	*giovedì*	jo·ve·*dee*
Friday	*venerdì*	ve·ner·*dee*
Saturday	*sabato*	*sa*·ba·to
Sunday	*domenica*	do·*me*·nee·ka

January	*gennaio*	je·*na*·yo
February	*febbraio*	fe·*bra*·yo
March	*marzo*	*mar*·tso
April	*aprile*	a·*pree*·le
May	*maggio*	*ma*·jo
June	*giugno*	*joo*·nyo
July	*luglio*	*loo*·lyo
August	*agosto*	a·*gos*·to
September	*settembre*	se·*tem*·bre
October	*ottobre*	o·*to*·bre
November	*novembre*	no·*vem*·bre
December	*dicembre*	dee·*chem*·bre

spring	*primavera*	pree·ma·*ve*·ra
summer	*estate*	es·*ta*·te
autumn	*autunno*	ow·*too*·no
winter	*inverno*	een·*ver*·no

What date is it today?
Che giorno è oggi? ke *jor*·no e *o*·jee

It's (15 December).
È (il quindici) e (eel *kween*·dee·chee
dicembre). dee·*chem*·bre)

last ...

night	*ieri notte*	ye·ree *no*·te
week	*la settimana scorsa*	la se·tee·*ma*·na *skor*·sa
month	*il mese scorso*	eel *me*·ze *skor*·so
year	*l'anno scorso*	*la*·no *skor*·so

next ...

week	*la settimana prossima*	la se·tee·*ma*·na *pro*·see·ma
month	*il mese prossimo*	eel *me*·ze *pro*·see·mo
year	*l'anno prossimo*	*la*·no *pro*·see·mo

since (May) *da (maggio)* da (*ma*·jo)

tomorrow ... *domani ...* do·*ma*·nee ...

morning	*mattina*	ma·*tee*·na
afternoon	*pomeriggio*	po·me·*ree*·jo
evening	*sera*	*se*·ra

yesterday ... *ieri ...* *ye*·ree ...

morning	*mattina*	ma·*tee*·na
afternoon	*pomeriggio*	po·me·*ree*·jo
evening	*sera*	*se*·ra

A

aboard *a bordo* a bor-do
accident *incidente* m een-chee-*den*-te
accommodation *alloggio* m a-*lo*-jo
adaptor *spina* f *multipla* spee-na
    mool-tee-pla
address *indirizzo* m een-dee-*ree*-tso
admission price *prezzo* m *d'ingresso*
    pre-tso deen-*gre*-so
after *dopo* do-po
afternoon *pomeriggio* m po-me-ree-jo
aftershave *dopobarba* m do-po-*bar*-ba
again *di nuovo* dee nwo-vo
air-conditioned *ad aria condizionata* ad
    a-rya kon-dee-tsyo-na-ta
airline *linea* f *aerea* lee-ne-a a-*e*-re-a
airport *aeroporto* m a-e-ro-*por*-to
airport tax *tassa* f *aeroportuale* ta-sa
    a-e-ro-por-*twa*-le
aisle (plane, train) *corridoio* m
    ko-ree-*do*-yo
alarm clock *sveglia* f *sve*-lya
alcohol *alcol* m *al*-kol
all (plural) *tutti/e* m/f too-tee/too-te
all (singular) *tutto/a* m/f too-to/a
allergy *allergia* f a-ler-*jee*-a
ambulance *ambulanza* f am-boo-*lan*-tsa
and *e* e
ankle *caviglia* f ka-*vee*-lya
antibiotics *antibiotici* m pl
    an-tee-*bee*-o-tee-chee
antique *pezzo* m *di antiquariato* pe-tso dee
    an-tee-kwa-*rya*-to
antiseptic *antisettico* m an-tee-*se*-tee-ko
appointment *appuntamento* m
    a-poon-ta-*men*-to
archaeological *archeologico/a* m/f
    ar-ke-o-*lo*-jee-ko/a

architect *architetto* m ar-kee-*te*-to
architecture *architettura* f ar-kee-te-*too*-ra
arm *braccio* m *bra*-cho
arrivals *arrivi* m pl a-*ree*-vee
art *arte* f *ar*-te
art gallery *galleria* f *d'arte* ga-le-*ree*-a
    dar-te
artist *artista* m&f ar-*tee*-sta
ashtray *portacenere* m por-ta-*che*-ne-re
at *a* a
aunt *zia* f tsee-a
Australia *Australia* f ow-*stra*-lya
automatic teller machine (ATM)
    Bancomat m ban-ko-mat
awful *orrendo/a* m/f o-*ren*-do/a

B

B&W (film) *in bianco e nero* een *byan*-ko
    e *ne*-ro
baby *bimbo/a* m/f *beem*-bo/a
baby food *cibo* m *da bebè* chee-bo da be-*be*
back (body) *schiena* f *skye*-na
backpack *zaino* m *dzai*-no
bad *cattivo/a* m/f ka-*tee*-vo/a
bag (general) *borsa* f *bor*-sa
bag (shopping) *sacchetto* m sa-*ke*-to
baggage *bagaglio* m ba-*ga*-lyo
baggage allowance *bagaglio* m *consentito*
    ba-*ga*-lyo kon-sen-*tee*-to
baggage claim *ritiro* m *bagagli* ree-*tee*-ro
    ba-*ga*-lyee
bakery *panetteria* f pa-ne-te-*ree*-a
band (music) *gruppo* m *groo*-po
bandage *fascia* f *fa*-sha
Band-aids *cerotti* m pl che-*ro*-tee
bank (money) *banca* f *ban*-ka
bank account *conto* m *in banca* con-to
    een *ban*-ka

B English–Italian dictionary

banknote *banconota* f ban-ko-*no*-ta
bar *locale* m lo-*ka*-le
bath *bagno* m *ba*-nyo
bathroom *bagno* m *ba*-nyo
battery *pila* f *pee*-la
beach *spiaggia* f *spya*-ja
beautiful *bello/a* m/f be-*lo*/a
beauty salon *parrucchiere* m pa-roo-*kye*-re
because *perché* per-*ke*
bed *letto* m *le*-to
bedroom *camera* f *da letto* *ka*-me-ra da *le*-to
beer *birra* f *bee*-ra
before *prima* *pree*-ma
behind *dietro* *dye*-tro
best *migliore* mee-*lyo*-re
better *migliore* mee-*lyo*-re
bicycle *bicicletta* f bee-chee-*kle*-ta
big *grande* *gran*-de
bill (account) *conto* m *kon*-to
birthday *compleanno* m kom-ple-*a*-no
black *nero/a* m/f *ne*-ro/a
blanket *coperta* f ko-*per*-ta
blister *vescica* f ve-*shee*-ka
blocked *bloccato/a* m/f blo-*ka*-to/a
blood *sangue* m *san*-gwe
blood group *gruppo sanguigno* *groo*-po *san-gwee*-nyo
blue (dark) *blu* bloo
blue (light) *azzurro* m/f a-*dzoo*-ro/a
board (a plane, ship) *salire su* sa-*lee*-re su
boarding house *pensione* f pen-*syo*-ne
boarding pass *carta f d'imbarco* *kar*-ta deem-*bar*-ko
boat *barca* f *bar*-ka
book *libro* m *lee*-bro
book (make a booking) *prenotare* pre-no-*ta*-re
booked out *completo/a* m/f kom-*ple*-to/a
bookshop *libreria* f lee-bre-*ree*-a
boots *stivali* m pl stee-*va*-lee
border *confine* m kon-*fee*-ne

boring *noioso/a* m/f no-*yo*-zo/a
bottle *bottiglia* f bo-*tee*-lya
bottle opener *apribottiglie* m a-pree-bo-*tee*-lye
bowl *piatto m fondo* *pya*-to *fon*-do
box *scatola* f *ska*-to-la
boy *bambino* m bam-*bee*-no
boy(friend) *ragazzo* m ra-*ga*-tso
bra *reggiseno* m re-jee-*se*-no
bread *pane* m *pa*-ne
breakfast *(prima) colazione* f (*pree*-ma) ko-la-*tsyo*-ne
bridge *ponte* m *pon*-te
briefcase *valigetta* f va-lee-*je*-ta
broken *rotto/a* m/f *ro*-to/a
broken down *guastato/a* m/f gwas-*ta*-to/a
brother *fratello* m fra-*te*-lo
brown *marrone* m/f ma-*ro*-ne
budget *bilancio* m bee-*lan*-cho
buffet (meal) *pasto m freddo* *pas*-to *fre*-do
building *edificio* m e-dee-*fee*-cho
bum *culo* m *koo*-lo
burn *bruciare* broo-*cha*-re
bus (city) *autobus* m *ow*-to-boos
bus (coach) *pullman* m *pool*-man
bus station *stazione f d'autobus* sta-*tsyo*-ne *dow*-to-boos
bus stop *fermata f d'autobus* fer-*ma*-ta *dow*-to-boos
business *affari* m pl a-*fa*-ree
business class *classe f business* *kla*-se *beez*-nes
business person *uomo/donna d'affari* m/f *wo*-mo/*do*-na da-*fa*-ree
business trip *viaggio m d'affari* vee-*a*-jo da-*fa*-ree
butcher's shop *macelleria* f ma-che-le-*ree*-a
button *bottone* m bo-*to*-ne
buy *comprare* kom-*pra*-re

C

café *bar* m bar
calculator *calcolatrice* f kal·ko·la·*tree*·che
camera *macchina* f *fotografica* ma·kee·na
  fo·to·*gra*·fee·ka
camp site *campeggio* m kam·*pe*·jo
can (tin) *scatola* f *ska*·to·la
can opener *apriscatole* m a·pree·*ska*·to·le
Canada *Canada* m *ka*·na·da
cancel *cancellare* kan·che·*la*·re
car *macchina* f ma·kee·na
car hire *autonoleggio* m ow·to·no·*le*·jo
car owner's title *libretto* m *di circolazione*
  lee·*bre*·to dee cheer·ko·la·*tsyo*·ne
car registration *bollo* m *di circolazione*
  bo·lo dee cheer·ko·la·*tsyo*·ne
cash *soldi* m pl *sol*·dee
cash register *cassa* f *ka*·sa
cashier *cassiere/a* m/f ka·sye·re/a
cassette *cassetta* f ka·se·ta
castle *castello* m kas·*te*·lo
cathedral *duomo* m *dwo*·mo
CD *cid* m chee·dee
centimetre *centimetro* m chen·*tee*·me·tro
centre *centro* m *chen*·tro
chair *sedia* f se·dya
chairlift (skiing) *seggiovia* f se·jo·vee·a
change *cambiare* kam·*bya*·re
change (coins) *spiccioli* m pl *spee*·cho·lee
change (money) *resto* m *res*·to
change room (sport) *spogliatoio* m
  spo·lya·*to*·yo
cheap *economico/a* m/f e·ko·*no*·mee·ko/a
check *controllare* kon·tro·*la*·re
check (bill) *conto* m *kon*·to
check-in (airport) *accetazione* f
  a·che·ta·*tsyo*·ne
check-in (hotel) *registrazione* f
  re·jee·stra·*tsyo*·ne

cheese *formaggio* m for·*ma*·jo
chef *cuoco/a* m/f *kwo*·ko/a
chemist *farmacista* m&f far·ma·*chee*·sta
cheque *assegno* m a·se·nyo
chest *petto* m *pe*·to
chicken *pollo* m *po*·lo
child *bambino/a* m/f bam·*bee*·no/a
child seat *seggiolino* m se·jo·*lee*·no
chocolate *cioccolato* m cho·ko·*la*·to
Christmas *Natale* m na·*ta*·le
church *chiesa* f *kye*·za
cigar *sigaro* m *see*·ga·ro
cigarette *sigaretta* f see·ga·*re*·ta
cigarette lighter *accendino* m
  a·chen·*dee*·no
cinema *cinema* m *chee*·ne·ma
circus *circo* m *cheer*·ko
city *città* f chee·*ta*
classical *classico/a* m/f *kla*·see·ko/a
clean *pulito/a* m/f poo·*lee*·to/a
cleaning *pulizia* f poo·lee·*tsee*·a
client *cliente* m&f klee·*en*·te
cloakroom *guardaroba* m gwar·da·*ro*·ba
closed *chiuso/a* m/f *kyoo*·zo/a
clothing *abbigliamento* m
  a·*bee*·lya·men·to
clothing store *negozio* m *di abbigliamento*
  ne·*go*·tsyo dee a·*bee*·lya·men·to
coat *cappotto* m ka·*po*·to
coffee *caffè* m ka·*fe*
coins *monete* f pl mo·*ne*·te
cold *freddo/a* m/f *fre*·do/a
colleague *collega* m&f ko·*le*·ga
collect call *chiamata* f *a carico del*
  destinatario kya·*ma*·ta a *ka*·ree·ko del
  des·tee·na·*ta*·ryo
colour *colore* m ko·*lo*·re
comb *pettine* m *pe*·tee·ne
comfortable *comodo/a* m/f *ko*·mo·do/a

commission *commissione* f ko·mee·*syo*·ne

companion *compagno/a* m/f kom·*pa*·nyo/a

company (firm) *ditta* f *dee*·ta

complain *lamentarsi* la·men·*tar*·see

complimentary (free) *gratuito/a* m/f gra·*too*·ee·to/a

computer *computer* m kom·*pyoo*·ter

concert *concerto* m kon·*cher*·to

conditioner *balsamo* m *per i capelli* *bal*·sa·mo per ee ka·*pe*·lee

condom *preservativo* m pre·zer·va·*tee*·vo

confirm (a booking) *confermare* kon·fer·*ma*·re

connection (transport) *coincidenza* f ko·een·chee·*den*·tsa

constipation *stitichezza* f stee·tee·*ke*·tsa

consulate *consolato* m kon·so·*la*·to

contact lenses *lenti* f pl *a contatto* *len*·tee a kon·*ta*·to

convenience store *alimentari* m a·lee·men·*ta*·ree

cook *cuoco/a* m/f *kwo*·ko/a

cook *cucinare* koo·chee·*na*·re

cost *costare* kos·*ta*·re

cotton balls *batuffoli* m pl *di cotone* ba·*too*·fo·lee dee ko·*to*·ne

cough *tossire* to·*see*·re

cough medicine *sciroppo* m *per la tosse* shee·*ro*·po per la *to*·se

countryside *campagna* f kam·*pa*·nya

court (tennis) *campo* m *da tennis* *kam*·po da te·nees

cover charge (restaurant) *coperto* m ko·*per*·to

cover charge (venue) *ingresso* m een·*gre*·so

craft (product) *pezzo* m *d'artigianato* *pe*·tso dar·tee·ja·*na*·to

craft (trade) *mestiere* m mes·*tye*·re

cream (food) *panna* f *pa*·na

credit card *carta* f *di credito* *kar*·ta dee *kre*·dee·to

cup *tazza* f *ta*·tsa

currency exchange *cambio* m *valuta* *kam*·byo va·*loo*·ta

current (electricity) *corrente* m ko·*ren*·te

customs *dogana* f do·*ga*·na

cut *tagliare* ta·*lya*·re

cutlery *posate* f pl po·*za*·te

D

dance *ballare* ba·*la*·re

dancing *ballo* m *ba*·lo

dangerous *pericoloso/a* m/f pe·ree·ko·*lo*·zo/a

dark *scuro/a* m/f *skoo*·ro/a

date (day) *data* f *da*·ta

date of birth *data* f *di nascita* *da*·ta dee *na*·shee·ta

daughter *figlia* f *fee*·lya

day *giorno* m *jor*·no

day after tomorrow *dopodomani* do·po·do·*ma*·nee

day before yesterday *altro ieri* m al·tro *ye*·ree

delay *ritardo* m ree·*tar*·do

delicatessen *salumeria* f sa·loo·me·*ree*·a

dental floss *filo* m *dentario* *fee*·lo den·*ta*·ree·o

dentist *dentista* m&f den·*tee*·sta

deodorant *deodorante* m de·o·do·*ran*·te

depart *partire* par·*tee*·re

department store *grande magazzino* m *gran*·de ma·ga·*dzee*·no

departure *partenza* f par·*ten*·tsa

dessert *dolce* m *dol*·che

destination *destinazione* f des·tee·na·*tsyo*·ne

diabetes *diabete* m dee·a·*be*·te

dial tone *segnale* m (*acustico*) se·*nya*·le (a·*koos*·tee·ko)

diaper *pannolino* m pa·no·*lee*·no

diarrhoea *diarrea* f dee·a·*re*·a

diary *agenda* f a·*jen*·da

dictionary *vocabolario* m vo·ka·bo·*la*·ryo

different *diverso/a* m/f dee·*ver*·so/a

dining car *carrozza* f *ristorante* ka·ro·*tsa* rees·to·*ran*·te

dinner *cena* f *che*·na

direct *diretto/a* m/f dee·*re*·to/a

direct-dial *telefono* m *diretto* te·*le*·fo·no dee·*re*·to

direction *direzione* f dee·re·*tsyo*·ne

dirty *sporco/a* m/f *spor*·ko/a

disabled *disabile* dee·*za*·bee·le

discount *sconto* m *skon*·to

disk (computer) *dischetto* m dees·*ke*·to

divorced *divorziato/a* m/f dee·vor·*tsya*·to/a

doctor *medico* m *me*·dee·ko

dog *cane* m *ka*·ne

dollar *dollaro* m *do*·la·ro

dope (drugs) *roba* f *ro*·ba

double bed *letto* m *matrimoniale* *le*·to ma·tree·mo·*nya*·le

double room *camera* f *doppia* ka·mer·a *do*·pya

down *giù* joo

dress *abito* m a·*bee*·to

drink *bere* *be*·re

drive *guidare* gwee·*da*·re

drivers licence *patente* f (*di guida*) pa·*ten*·te (dee *gwee*·da)

drunk *ubriaco/a* m/f oo·bree·a·ko/a

dry *secco/a* m/f se·ko/a

dry *asciugare* a·shoo·ga·re

dummy (pacifier) *ciucciotto* m choo·*cho*·to

E

each *ciascuno/a* m/f chas·*koo*·no/a

ear *orecchio* m o·re·kyo

early *presto* m/f *pres*·to

earrings *orecchini* m pl o·re·*kee*·nee

east *est* m est

Easter *Pasqua* f *pas*·kwa

economy class *classe* f *turistica* kla·se too·ree·stee·ka

electricity *elettricità* f e·le·tree·chee·*ta*

elevator *ascensore* m a·shen·*so*·re

email *email* m e·mayl

embassy *ambasciata* f am·ba·*sha*·ta

emergency *emergenza* f e·mer·*jen*·tsa

empty *vuoto/a* m/f *vwo*·to/a

end *fine* f *fee*·ne

end *finire* fee·*nee*·re

engagement (couple) *fidanzamento* m fee·dan·tsa·*men*·to

engine *motore* m mo·*to*·re

engineer *ingegnere* m&f een·je·*nye*·re

England *Inghilterra* f een·geel·*te*·ra

English *inglese* een·*gle*·ze

enough *abbastanza* a·bas·*tan*·tsa

enter *entrare* en·*tra*·re

entertainment guide *guida* f *agli spettacoli* *gwee*·da a·lyee spe·*ta*·ko·lee

entry *entrata* f en·*tra*·ta

escalator *scala* f *mobile* ska·la *mo*·bee·le

euro *euro* m e·*oo*·ro

Europe *Europa* f e·oo·*ro*·pa

evening *sera* f *se*·ra

everything *tutto* m *too*·to

exchange *cambiare* kam·*bya*·re

exchange rate *tasso* m *di cambio* ta·so dee *kam*·byo

exhibition *esposizione* f es·po·zee·*tsyo*·ne

exit *uscita* f oo·*shee*·ta

expensive *caro/a* m/f ka-ro/a
express *espresso/a* m/f es-pre-so/a
express mail *posta prioritaria* pos-ta pree-o-ree-ta-rya
eye *occhio* m o-kyo

F

face *faccia* f fa-cha
fall (autumn) *autunno* m ow-too-no
family *famiglia* f fa-mee-lya
family name *cognome* m ko-nyo-me
fan (machine) *ventilatore* m ven-tee-la-to-re
fan (person) *tifoso/a* m/f tee-fo-zo/a
far *lontano/a* m/f lon-ta-no/a
fashion *moda* f mo-da
fast *veloce* ve-lo-che
fat *grasso/a* m/f gra-so/a
father *padre* m pa-dre
father-in-law *suocero* m swo-che-ro
faucet *rubinetto* m roo-bee-ne-to
faulty *difettoso/a* m/f dee-fe-to-zo/a
fax *fax* m faks
feel *sentire* sen-tee-re
ferry *traghetto* m tra-ge-to
fever *febbre* f fe-bre
fiancé(e) *fidanzato/a* m/f fee-dan-tsa-to/a
film (cinema) *film* m feelm
film speed *ASA* a-za
fine (payment) *multa* f mool-ta
finger *dito* m dee-to
first class *prima classe* f pree-ma kla-se
first-aid kit *valigetta f del pronto soccorso* va-lee-je-ta del pron-to so-kor-so
fish shop *pescheria* f pe-ske-ree-a
fishing *pesca* f pe-ska
flash (camera) *flash* m flesh
flashlight (torch) *torcia f elettrica* tor-cha e-le-tree-ka

flight *volo* m vo-lo
floor (storey) *piano* m pya-no
florist *fioraio* m&f fyo-ra-yo
flu *influenza* f een-floo-en-tsa
fly *volare* vo-la-re
food *cibo* m chee-bo
food supplies *provviste* m pl *alimentari* pro-vee-ste a-lee-men-ta-ree
foot *piede* m pye-de
football (soccer) *calcio* m kal-cho
footpath *marciapiede* m mar-cha-pye-de
foreign *straniero/a* m/f stra-nye-ro/a
forest *foresta* f fo-res-ta
fork *forchetta* f for-ke-ta
fortnight *quindici giorni* m pl kween-dee-chee jor-nee
fragile *fragile* fra-jee-le
France *Francia* f fran-cha
free (gratis) *gratuito/a* m/f gra-too-ee-to/a
fresh *fresco/a* m/f fres-ko/a
fridge *frigorifero* m free-go-ree-fe-ro
friend *amico/a* m/f a-mee-ko/a
frozen *congelato/a* m/f kon-je-la-to/a
fruit *frutta* f froo-ta
fry *friggere* free-je-re
frying pan *padella* f pa-de-la
full *pieno/a* m/f pye-no/a
funny *divertente* dee-ver-ten-te
furniture *mobili* m pl mo-bee-lee

G

game (play) *gioco* m jo-ko
game (sport) *partita* f par-tee-ta
garden *giardino* m jar-dee-no
gas (for cooking) *gas* m gaz
gas (petrol) *benzina* f ben-dzee-na
gastroenteritis *gastroenterite* f gas-tro-en-te-ree-te

gay *gay* gei
Germany *Germania* f jer·*ma*·nya
gift *regalo* m re·*ga*·lo
girl(friend) *ragazza* f ra·*ga*·tsa
glasses (spectacles) *occhiali* m pl o·*kya*·lee
gloves *guanti* m pl *gwan*·tee
go *andare* an·*da*·re
gold *oro* m *o*·ro
golf course *campo* m *da golf* *kam*·po da golf
good *buono/a* m/f *bwo*·no/a
grandchild *nipote* m&f nee·*po*·te
grandfather *nonno* m *no*·no
grandmother *nonna* f *no*·na
great *ottimo/a* m/f o·tee·mo/a
green *verde* ver·de
grey *grigio/a* m/f *gree*·jo/a
grocery *drogheria* f dro·ge·*ree*·a
guesthouse *pensione* f pen·*syo*·ne
guide (person) *guida* f *gwee*·da
guidebook *guida* f *(turistica)* *gwee*·da (too·*ree*·stee·ka)
guided tour *visita* f *guidata* vee·zee·ta gwee·*da*·ta
gym *palestra* f pa·*le*·stra

H

hairdresser *parrucchiere/a* m/f pa·roo·*kye*·re/a
hand *mano* f *ma*·no
handbag *borsetta* f bor·*se*·ta
handicrafts *oggetti* m pl *d'artigianato* o·*je*·tee dar·tee·ja·*na*·to
handkerchief *fazzoletto* m fa·tso·*le*·to
handmade *fatto/a* m/f *a mano* fa·to/a a *ma*·no
handsome *bello/a* m/f *be*·lo/a
happy *felice* m/f fe·*lee*·che
hard (not soft) *duro/a* m/f *doo*·ro/a

hat *cappello* m ka·*pe*·lo
have *avere* a·*ve*·re
hay fever *febbre* f *da fieno* *fe*·bre da *fye*·no
he *lui* *loo*·ee
head *testa* f *tes*·ta
headache *mal* m *di testa* mal dee *tes*·ta
headlights *fari* m pl *fa*·ree
heart *cuore* m *kwo*·re
heart condition *problema* m *cardiaco* pro·*ble*·ma kar·*dee*·a·ko
heat *caldo* m *kal*·do
heater *stufa* f *stoo*·fa
heavy *pesante* pe·*zan*·te
help *aiutare* a·yoo·*ta*·re
here *qui* kwee
high *alto/a* m/f *al*·to/a
hike *escursione* f *a piedi* es·koor·*syo*·ne a *pye*·de
hiking *escursionismo* m *a piedi* es·koor·syo·*neez*·mo a *pye*·de
hire *noleggiare* no·le·*ja*·re
hitchhike *fare l'autostop* fa·re low·to·stop
holidays *vacanze* f pl va·*kan*·tse
home *casa* f *ka*·za
homosexual *omosessuale* m&f o·mo·se·*swa*·le
honeymoon *luna* f *di miele* *loo*·na dee *mye*·le
horse riding *andare a cavallo* an·*da*·re a ka·*va*·lo
hospital *ospedale* m os·pe·*da*·le
hot *caldo/a* m/f *kal*·do/a
hotel *albergo* m al·*ber*·go
hour *ora* f *o*·ra
husband *marito* m ma·*ree*·to

I

ice *ghiaccio* m *gya*·cho
ice cream *gelato* m je·*la*·to

identification *documento* m *d'identità*
do-koo-*men*-to dee-den-*tee*-ta

identification card (ID) *carta* f *d'identità*
kar-ta dee-den-*tee*-ta

ill *malato/a* m/f ma-*la*-to/a

important *importante* eem-por-*tan*-te

impossible *impossibile* eem-po-*see*-bee-le

included *compreso/a* m/f kom-*pre*-zo/a

indigestion *indigestione* f
een-dee-je-*styo*-ne

infection *infezione* f een-fe-*tsyo*-ne

influenza *influenza* f een-floo-*en*-tsa

information *informazioni* f pl
een-for-ma-*tsyo*-nee

injection *iniezione* f ee-nye-*tsyo*-ne

injured *ferito/a* m/f fe-*ree*-to/a

injury *ferita* f fe-*ree*-ta

insurance *assicurazione* f
a-see-koo-ra-*tsyo*-ne

intermission *intervallo* m een-ter-*va*-lo

Internet (café) *Internet (point)* m
een-ter-net (poynt)

interpreter *interprete* m/f een-*ter*-pre-te

Ireland *Irlanda* f eer-*lan*-da

iron (for clothes) *ferro* m *da stiro* fe-ro
da *stee*-ro

island *isola* f *ee*-zo-la

IT *informatica* f een-for-*ma*-tee-ka

itch *prurito* m proo-*ree*-to

itinerary *itinerario* m ee-tee-ne-*ra*-ryo

J

jacket *giacca* f *ja*-ka

jeans *jeans* m pl jeens

jet lag *disturbi* m pl *da fuso orario*
dees-*toor*-bee da *foo*-zo o-*ra*-ryo

jewellery *gioielli* m pl jo-*ye*-lee

job *lavoro* m la-*vo*-ro

journalist *giornalista* m&f jor-na-*lee*-sta

jumper *maglione* f ma-*lyo*-ne

K

kilogram *chilo* m *kee*-lo

kilometre *chilometro* m kee-*lo*-me-tro

kind *gentile* jen-*tee*-le

kitchen *cucina* f koo-*chee*-na

knee *ginocchio* m jee-*no*-kyo

knife *coltello* m kol-*te*-lo

L

lake *lago* m *la*-go

language *lingua* f *leen*-gwa

laptop (computer) *portatile* m
(kom-*pyoo*-ter) por-*ta*-tee-le

last *ultimo/a* m/f *ool*-tee-mo/a

late *in ritardo* een ree-*tar*-do

laundrette *lavanderia* f *a gettone*
la-van-de-*ree*-a je-*to*-ne

laundry *lavanderia* f la-van-de-*ree*-a

law *legge* f *le*-je

lawyer *avvocato/a* m/f a-vo-*ka*-to/a

laxatives *lassativi* m pl la-sa-*tee*-vee

leather *cuoio* m *kwo*-yo

left (direction) *sinistra* f see-*nee*-stra

left luggage (office) *deposito* m *bagagli*
de-*po*-zee-to ba-*ga*-lyee

leg *gamba* f *gam*-ba

lens *obiettivo* m o-bye-*tee*-vo

lesbian *lesbica* f *lez*-bee-ka

less (di) *meno* (dee) *me*-no

letter *lettera* f *le*-te-ra

library *biblioteca* f bee-blyo-*te*-ka

life jacket *giubbotto* m *di salvataggio*
joo-*bo*-to dee sal-va-*ta*-jo

lift (elevator) *ascensore* m a-shen-*so*-re

LOOK UP

light *luce* f *loo·*che
light (colour) *chiaro/a* m/f *kya·*ro/a
light (not heavy) *leggero/a* m/f le·*je·*ro/a
light meter *esposimetro* m
  es·po·zee·me·tro
lighter *accendino* m a·chen·*dee·*no
like *piacere* pya·*che·*re
lipstick *rossetto* m ro·*se·*to
liquor store *bottiglieria* f bo·tee·lye·*ree·*a
listen *ascoltare* as·kol·*ta·*re
local *locale* lo·*ka·*le
locked *chiuso/a* m/f *(a chiave)* kyoo·zo/a
  (a *kya·*ve)
long *lungo/a* m/f *loon·*go/a
lost *perso/a* m/f *per·*so/a
loud *forte* m/f *for·*te
love *amare* a·*ma·*re
lubricant *lubrificante* m
  loo·bree·fee·*kan·*te
luggage *bagaglio* m ba·*ga·*lyo
luggage lockers *armadietti* m pl *per i
  bagagli* ar·ma·*dye·*tee per ee ba·*ga·*lyee
lunch *pranzo* m *pran·*dzo

M

mail *posta* f *pos·*ta
mail box *buca* f *delle lettere* *boo·*ka de·le
  *le·*te·re
make-up *trucco* m *troo·*ko
man *uomo* m *wo·*mo
manager *manager* m *me·*nee·je
map *pianta* f *pyan·*ta
market *mercato* m mer·*ka·*to
married *sposato/a* m/f spo·*za·*to/a
massage *massaggio* m ma·*sa·*jo
match (sport) *partita* f par·*tee·*ta
matches *fiammiferi* m pl fya·*me·*fe·ree
meat *carne* f *kar·*ne

medicine *medicina* f me·dee·*chee·*na
menu *menu* m me·*noo*
message *messaggio* m me·*sa·*jo
metro station *stazione* f *della
  metropolitana* sta·*tsyo·*ne de·la
  me·tro·po·lee·*ta·*na
microwave oven *forno* m *a microonde*
  *for·*no a mee·kro·on·de
midnight *mezzanotte* f me·dza *no·*te
milk *latte* m *la·*te
millimetre *millimetro* m mee·*lee·*me·tro
mineral water *acqua* f *minerale* a·kwa
  mee·ne·*ra·*le
minute *minuto* m mee·*noo·*to
mirror *specchio* m *spe·*kyo
mobile phone *(telefono) cellulare* m
  (te·*le·*fo·no) che·loo·*la·*re
modem *modem* m *mo·*dem
modern *moderno/a* m/f mo·*der·*no/a
money *denaro* m de·*na·*ro
month *mese* m *me·*ze
more *(di) più* (dee) *pyoo*
morning *mattina* f ma·*tee·*na
mother *madre* f *ma·*dre
mother-in-law *suocera* f *swo·*che·ra
motorway (tollway) *autostrada* f
  ow·to·stra·da
mountain *montagna* f mon·*ta·*nya
mouth *bocca* f *bo·*ka
movie *film* m feelm
museum *museo* m moo·*ze·*o
music *musica* f *moo·*zee·ka

N

nail clippers *tagliaunghie* m ta·lya·*oon·*gye
name *nome* m *no·*me
napkin *tovagliolo* m to·va·*lyo·*lo
nappy *pannolino* m pa·no·*lee·*no

near (to) *vicino (a)* vee-*chee*-no (a)
nearby *vicino/a* m/f vee-*chee*-no/a
needle (sewing) *ago* m a-go
needle (syringe) *ago* m *da siringa* a-go da see-*reen*-ga
Netherlands *Paesi Bassi* m pl pa-e-zee *ba*-see
new *nuovo/a* m/f nwo-vo/a
New Year's Day *Capodanno* m *ka*-po *da*-no
New Year's Eve *san Silvestro* m san seel-*ves*-tro
New Zealand *Nuova Zelanda* f nwo-va dze-*lan*-da
news *notizie* f pl no-*tee*-tsye
newsagency *edicola* f e-*dee*-ko-la
newspaper *giornale* m jor-*na*-le
next *prossimo/a* m/f pro-*see*-mo/a
night *notte* f *no*-te
no *no* no
noisy *rumoroso/a* m/f roo-mo-*ro*-zo/a
nonsmoking *non fumatore* non foo-ma-*to*-re
north *nord* m nord
notebook *quaderno* m kwa-*der*-no
nothing *niente* nyen-te
now *adesso* a-*de*-so
number *numero* m *noo*-me-ro
nurse *infermiere/a* m/f een-fer-*mye*-re/a

O

ocean *oceano* m o-*che*-a-no
oil *olio* m o-lyo
on *su* soo
one-way (ticket) *(un biglietto di) solo andata* (oon bee-*lye*-to dee) so-lo an-*da*-ta
only *solo* so-lo
open *aperto/a* m/f a-*per*-to/a
open *aprire* a-*pree*-re

opening hours *orario* m *di apertura* o-*ra*-ryo dee a-per-*too*-ra
orange (colour) *arancione* a-ran-*cho*-ne
other *altro/a* m/f al-tro/a
outside *fuori* fwo-ree

P

pacifier *ciucciotto* m choo-*cho*-to
packet (general) *pacchetto* m pa-*ke*-to
padlock *lucchetto* m loo-*ke*-to
pain *dolore* m do-*lo*-re
painful *doloroso/a* m/f do-lo-*ro*-zo/a
painkillers *analgesico* m an-al-*je*-zee-ko
painter *pittore/pittrice* m/f pee-*to*-re/pee-*tree*-che
painting (the art) *pittura* f pee-*too*-ra
palace *palazzo* m pa-*la*-tso
pants *pantaloni* m pl pan-ta-*lo*-nee
panty liners *salva slip* m pl *sal*-va sleep
pantyhose *collant* f pl ko-*lant*
paper *carta* f *kar*-ta
paperwork *moduli* m pl *mo*-doo-lee
parcel *pacchetto* m pa-*ke*-to
parents *genitori* m pl je-nee-*to*-ree
park *parco* m *par*-ko
party (celebration) *festa* f *fes*-ta
passenger *passeggero/a* m/f pa-se-*je*-ro/a
passport *passaporto* m pa-sa-*por*-to
path *sentiero* m sen-*tye*-ro
payment *pagamento* m pa-ga-*men*-to
pen (ballpoint) *penna* f *(a sfera)* pe-na (a *sfe*-ra)
pencil *matita* f ma-*tee*-ta
penis *pene* m *pe*-ne
penknife *temperino* m tem-pe-*ree*-no
pensioner *pensionato/a* m/f pen-syo-*na*-to/a
per (day) *al (giorno)* al (*jor*-no)

perfume *profumo* m pro-*foo*-mo
petrol *benzina* f ben-*dzee*-na
petrol station *distributore* m
  dee-stree-*boo*-to-re
pharmacy *farmacia* f far-ma-*chee*-a
phone book *elenco* m *telefonico* e-*len*-ko
  te-le-*fo*-nee-ko
phone box *cabina* f *telefonica* ka-*bee*-na
  te-le-*fo*-nee-ka
phone call *chiamata* f kya-*ma*-ta
photo *foto* f *fo*-to
photographer *fotografo* m *fo*-to-gra-fo
photography *fotografia* f fo-to-gra-*fee*-a
phrasebook *vocabularietto* m
  vo-ka-bo-la-*rye*-to
picnic *picnic* m *peek*-neek
pill *pillola* f *pee*-lo-la
pillow *cuscino* m koo-*shee*-no
pillowcase *federa* f *fe*-de-ra
pink *rosa* m/f *ro*-za
plane *aereo* m a-*e*-re-o
plate *piatto* m *pya*-to
platform *binario* m bee-*na*-ryo
play (theatre) *commedia* f ko-*me*-dya
plug (bath) *tappo* m *ta*-po
plug (electricity) *spina* f *spee*-na
point *indicare* een-dee-*ka*-re
police (civilian) *polizia* f po-lee-*tsee*-a
police (military) *carabinieri* m pl
  ka-ra-bee-*nye*-ree
police station *posto* m *di polizia* *pos*-to dee
  po-lee-*tsee*-a
pool (swimming) *piscina* f pee-*shee*-na
post code *codice* m *postale* ko-dee-che
  pos-ta-le
postoffice *ufficio* m *postale* oo-*fee*-cho
  pos-ta-le
postcard *cartolina* f kar-to-*lee*-na
pound (money) *sterlina* f ster-*lee*-na
pregnant *incinta* een-*cheen*-ta

prescription *ricetta* f ree-*che*-ta
present (gift) *regalo* m re-*ga*-lo
price *prezzo* m *pre*-tso
printer (computer) *stampante* f
  stam-*pan*-te
private *privato/a* m/f pree-*va*-to/a
pub *pub* m poob
public telephone *telefono* m *pubblico*
  te-*le*-fo-no poo-blee-ko
purple *viola* vee-*o*-la

Q

quiet *tranquillo/a* m/f tran-*kwee*-lo/a

R

rain *pioggia* f *pyo*-ja
raincoat *impermeabile* m
  eem-per-me-*a*-bee-le
rare *raro/a* m/f *ra*-ro/a
razor *rasoio* m *(elettrico)* ra-*zo*-yo
  (e-*le*-tree-ko)
razor blades *lamette* f pl *(da barba)*
  la-*me*-te (da *bar*-ba)
receipt *ricevuta* f ree-che-*voo*-ta
recommend *raccomandare*
  ra-ko-man-*da*-re
red *rosso/a* m/f *ro*-so/a
refrigerator *frigo* m *free*-go
refund *rimborso* m reem-*bor*-so
registered mail *(posta)* *raccomandata* f
  (pos-ta) ra-ko-man-*da*-ta
remote control *telecomando* m
  te-le-ko-*man*-do
repair *riparare* ree-pa-*ra*-re
reservation *prenotazione* f
  pre-no-ta-*tsyo*-ne
restaurant *ristorante* m rees-to-*ran*-te

return (ticket) (biglietto) di andata e ritorno (bee-lye-to) dee an-da-ta e ree-tor-no
right (direction) a destra a de-stra
river fiume m fyoo-me
rock (music) (musica) f rock (moo-zee-ka) rok
romantic romantico/a m/f ro-man-tee-ko/a
room camera f ka-me-ra
ruins rovine f pl ro-vee-ne

S

safe sicuro/a m/f see-koo-ro/a
safe sex rapporti m pl protetti ra-por-tee pro-te-tee
sanitary napkins assorbenti m pl igienici as-or-ben-tee ee-je-nee-chee
scarf sciarpa f shar-pa
science scienza f shen-tsa
scissors forbici f pl for-bee-chee
Scotland Scozia f sko-tsya
sculpture scultura f skool-too-ra
sea mare m ma-re
season stagione f sta-jo-ne
seat (place) posto m pos-to
seatbelt cintura (di sicurezza cheen-too-ra dee see-koo-re-tsa
second class seconda classe f se-kon-da kla-se
self-service self-service self-ser-vees
service servizio m ser-vee-tsyo
service charge servizio m ser-vee-tsyo
service station stazione f di servizio sta-tsyo-ne dee ser-vee-tsyo
sex sesso m se-so
shade ombra f om-bra
shape forma f for-ma
share (with) condividere kon-dee-vee-de-re
shave fare la barba fa-re la bar-ba

shaving cream crema f da barba kre-ma da bar-ba
sheet (bed) lenzuolo m len-tswo-lo
shirt camicia f ka-mee-cha
shoe shop negozio m di scarpe ne-go-tsyo dee skar-pe
shoes scarpe f pl skar-pe
shop negozio m ne-go-tsyo
shopping centre centro m commerciale chen-tro ko-mer-cha-le
short (height) basso/a m/f ba-so/a
short (length) corto/a m/f kor-to/a
shorts pantaloncini m pl pan-ta-lon-chee-nee
shoulder spalla f spa-la
show mostrare mos-tra-re
shower doccia f do-cha
shut chiuso/a m/f kyoo-zo/a
sick malato/a m/f ma-la-to/a
silk seta f se-ta
silver argento m ar-jen-to
single (man) celibe m che-lee-be
single (woman) nubile f noo-bee-le
single room camera f singola ka-me-ra seen-go-la
sister sorella f so-re-la
size (general) dimensioni f pl dee-men-syo-nee
skiing sci m shee
skirt gonna f go-na
sleep dormire dor-mee-re
sleeping bag sacco m a pelo sa-ko a pe-lo
sleeping car vagone m letto va-go-ne le-to
slice fetta f fe-ta
slide (film) diapositiva m dee-a-po-zee-tee-va
slowly lentamente len-ta-men-te
small piccolo/a m/f pee-ko-lo/a
smell odore m o-do-re
smoke fumare foo-ma-re

snack *spuntino* m spoon·*tee*·no

snow *neve* f *ne*·ve

soap *sapone* m sa·*po*·ne

socks *calzini* m pl cal·*tsee*·nee

some *alcuni/e* m/f al·*koo*·nee/al·*koo*·ne

son *figlio* m *fee*·lyo

soon *fra poco* fra *po*·ko

south *sud* m sood

souvenir *ricordino* m ree·kor·*dee*·no

souvenir shop *negozio* m *di souvenir*
ne·*go*·tsyo dee soo·ve·*neer*

Spain *Spagna* f *spa*·nya

speak *parlare* par·*la*·re

speed limit *limite* m *di velocità* lee·*mee*·te
dee ve·lo·chee·*ta*

spoon *cucchiaio* m koo·*kya*·yo

sports store *negozio* m *di articoli
sportivi* ne·*go*·tsyo dee ar·*tee*·ko·lee
spor·*tee*·vee

sprain *storta* f *stor*·ta

spring (season) *primavera* f pree·ma·*ve*·ra

square (town) *piazza* f *pya*·tsa

stairway *scale* f pl *ska*·le

stamp *francobollo* m fran·ko·*bo*·lo

standby (ticket) *(in lista) d'attesa* (een
lee·sta) da·*te*·za

station *stazione* f sta·*tsyo*·ne

stationer *cartolaio* m kar·to·*la*·yo

stockings *calze* f pl *kal*·tse

stolen *rubato/a* m/f roo·*ba*·to/a

stomach *stomaco* m *sto*·ma·ko

stomachache *mal* m *di pancia* mal dee
pan·cha

stop *fermare* fer·*ma*·re

student *studente/studentessa* m/f
stoo·*den*·te/stoo·den·*te*·sa

subway *metropolitana* f
me·tro·po·lee·*ta*·na

suitcase *valigia* f va·*lee*·ja

summer *estate* f es·*ta*·te

sun *sole* m *so*·le

sunblock *crema* f *solare* *kre*·ma so·*la*·re

sunburn *scottatura* f sko·ta·*too*·ra

sunglasses *occhiali* m pl *da sole* o·*kya*·lee
da *so*·le

sunscreen *crema* f *solare* *kre*·ma so·*la*·re

sunset *tramonto* m tra·*mon*·to

supermarket *supermercato* m
soo·per·mer·*ka*·to

surface mail *posta* f *ordinaria* pos·ta
or·dee·*na*·rya

surname *cognome* m ko·*nyo*·me

sweater *maglione* m ma·*lyo*·ne

sweet *dolce* *dol*·che

swim *nuotare* nwo·*ta*·re

swimming pool *piscina* f pee·*shee*·na

swimsuit *costume* m *da bagno* ko·*stoo*·me
da *ba*·nyo

T

tailor *sarto* m *sar*·to

take (photo) *fare* f *fa*·re

tampons *tamponi* m pl tam·*po*·nee

tanning lotion *lozione* f *abbronzante*
lo·*tsyo*·ne a·bron·*dzan*·te

tap (faucet) *rubinetto* m roo·bee·*ne*·to

tasty *gustoso/a* m/f goo·*sto*·zo/a

taxi *tassì* m ta·*see*

taxi stand *posteggio* m *di tassì* po·*ste*·jo
dee ta·*see*

tea *tè* m te

teaspoon *cucchiaino* m koo·kya·*ee*·no

telegram *telegramma* f te·le·*gra*·ma

telephone *telefono* m te·*le*·fo·no

telephone *telefonare* te·le·fo·*na*·re

television *televisione* f te·le·vee·*zyo*·ne

tennis *tennis* m *te*·nees

tennis court *campo* m *da tennis* kam·po da te·nees

theatre *teatro* m te·a·tro

there *là* la

this (one) *questo* a m/f kwe·sto/a

throat *gola* f go·la

ticket *biglietto* m bee·lye·to

ticket machine *distributore* m *automatico di biglietti* dee·stree·boo·to·re ow·to·ma·tee·ko dee bee·lye·tee

ticket office *biglietteria* f bee·lye·te·ree·a

time difference *differenza* f *di fuso orario* dee·fe·ren·tsa dee foo·zo o·ra·ryo

timetable *orario* m o·ra·ryo

tin (can) *scatoletta* f ska·to·le·ta

tin opener *apriscatole* m a·pree·ska·to·le

tip (gratuity) *mancia* f man·cha

tired *stanco/a* m/f stan·ko/a

tissues *fazzolettini* m pl *di carta* fa·tso·le·tee·nee dee kar·ta

toast *pane* m *tostato* pa·ne tos·ta·to

toaster *tostapane* m tos·ta·pa·ne

today *oggi* o·jee

together *insieme* een·sye·me

toilet *gabinetto* m ga·bee·ne·to

toilet paper *carta* f *igienica* kar·ta ee·je·nee·ka

tomorrow *domani* do·ma·nee

tonight *stasera* sta·se·ra

too (expensive) *troppo (caro/a)* tro·po (ka·ro/a)

toothache *mal* m *di denti* mal dee den·tee

toothbrush *spazzolino* m *da denti* spa·tso·lee·no da den·tee

toothpaste *dentifricio* m den·tee·free·cho

torch (flashlight) *torcia* f *elettrica* tor·cha e·le·tree·ka

tour *gita* f jee·ta

tourist *turista* m&f too·ree·sta

tourist office *ufficio* m *del turismo* oo·fee·cho del too·reez·mo

towel *asciugamano* m a·shoo·ga·ma·no

train *treno* m tre·no

train station *stazione* f *(ferroviaria)* sta·tsyo·ne (fe·ro·vyar·ya)

transit lounge *sala* f *di transito* sa·la dee tran·zee·to

translate *tradurre* tra·doo·re

travel agency *agenzia* f *di viaggio* a·jen·tsee·a dee vee·a·jo

travel sickness (air) *mal* m *di aereo* mal dee a·e·re·o

travel sickness (car) *mal* m *di macchina* mal dee ma·kee·na

travel sickness (sea) *mal* m *di mare* mal dee ma·re

travellers cheque *assegno* m *di viaggio* a·se·nyo dee vee·a·jo

trolley (luggage) *carrello* m ka·re·lo

trousers *pantaloni* m pl pan·ta·lo·nee

try *provare* pro·va·re

T-shirt *maglietta* f ma·lye·ta

TV *TV* f tee·voo

tweezers *pinzette* f pl peen·tse·te

twin beds *due letti* doo·e le·tee

twins *gemelli/e* m/f pl je·me·lee/je·me·le

tyre *gomma* f go·ma

U

umbrella *ombrello* m om·bre·lo

uncomfortable *scomodo/a* m/f sko·mo·do/a

underwear *biancheria* f *intima* byan·ke·ree·a een·tee·ma

university *università* f oo·nee·ver·see·ta

until *fino a* fee·no a

up *su* soo

urgent *urgente* m/f oor·jen·te

USA *Stati* m pl *Uniti d'America* sta·tee oo·nee·tee da·me·ree·ka

V

vacant *libero/a* m/f lee-be-ro/a
vacation *vacanza* f va-kan-tsa
vaccination *vaccinazione* f va-chee-na-tsyo-ne
vagina *vagina* f va-jee-na
validate *convalidare* kon-va-lee-da-re
valuable *prezioso/a* m/f pre-tsyo-zo/a
vegetable *verdura* f ver-doo-ra
vegetarian *vegetariano/a* m/f ve-je-ta-rya-no/a
video camera *videocamera* f vee-de-o-ka-me-ra
video tape *videonastro* m vee-de-o-nas-tro
view *vista* f vee-sta
visa *visto* m vee-sto

W

wait *aspettare* as-pe-ta-re
waiter *cameriere/a* m/f ka-mer-ye-re/a
waiting room *sala* f *d'attesa* sa-la da-te-sa
wake up *svegliarsi* sve-lyar-see
walk *passeggiata* f pa-se-ja-ta
walk *camminare* ka-mee-na-re
warm *tiepido/a* m/f tye-pee-do/a
wash (something) *lavare* la-va-re
washing machine *lavatrice* f la-va-tree-che
watch *guardare* gwar-da-re
water *acqua* f a-kwa
water bottle *borraccia* f bo-ra-cha
week *settimana* f se-tee-ma-na
weekend *fine* m *settimana* fee-ne se-tee-ma-na
west *ovest* m o-vest

wheelchair *sedia* f *a rotelle* se-dya a ro-te-le
when *quando* kwan-do
where *dove* do-ve
white *bianco/a* m/f byan-ko/a
who *chi* kee
why *perché* per-ke
wife *moglie* f mo-lye
window (car, plane) *finestrino* m fee-nes-tree-no
window (general) *finestra* f fee-nes-tra
wine *vino* m vee-no
wine cellar *cantina* f kan-tee-na
wine tasting *degustazione* f *dei vini* de-goos-ta-tsyo-ne day vee-nee
winery *cantina* f kan-tee-na
winter *inverno* m een-ver-no
without *senza* sen-tsa
woman *donna* f do-na
wool *lana* f la-na
write *scrivere* skree-ve-re

Y

year *anno* m a-no
yellow *giallo/a* m/f ja-lo/a
yes *sì* see
yesterday *ieri* ye-ree
you (inf) *tu* too
you (polite) *Lei* lay
youth hostel *ostello* m *della gioventù* os-te-lo de-la jo-ven-too

Z

zoo *giardino* m *zoologico* jar-dee-no dzo-o-lo-jee-ko

A

abbastanza a·bas·*tan*·tsa *enough*
abbigliamento m a·*bee*-lya-*men*-to *clothing*
abito m *a*·bee·to *dress*
accetazione f a·che·ta·*tsyo*·ne *check-in (airport)*
acqua f *a*·kwa *water*
acqua f **minerale** *ak*·wa me·ne·*ra*·le *mineral water*
adesso a·*de*·so *now*
aeroporto m a·e·ro·*por*·to *airport*
affari m pl a·*fa*·ree *business*
agenzia f **di viaggio** a·jen·*tsee*·a dee vee·a·jo *travel agency*
aiutare a·yoo·*ta*·re *help*
albergo m al·*ber*·go *hotel*
alloggio m a·*lo*·jo *accommodation*
altro ieri m ye·*ree* *day before yesterday*
ambasciata f am·ba·*sha*·ta *embassy*
amico/a m/f a·*mee*·ko/a *friend*
anno m *a*·no *year*
aperto/a m/f a·*per*·to/a *open*
appuntamento m a·poon·ta·*men*·to *appointment • date*
arancia f a·*ran*·cha *orange (fruit)*
arancione a·ran·*cho*·ne *orange (colour)*
aria f **condizionata** *a*·ree·a kon·dee·*tsyo*·na·ta *air conditioning*
armadietti m pl **per i bagagli** ar·ma·*dye*·tee per ee ba·*ga*·lyee *luggage lockers*
arrivi m pl a·*ree*·vee *arrivals*
assegno m **di viaggio** a·*se*·nyo dee vee·a·jo *travellers cheque*
assicurazione f a·see·koo·ra·*tsyo*·ne *insurance*
autobus m *ow*·to·boos *bus (city)*
autonoleggio m ow·to·no·*le*·jo *car hire*
azzurro/a m/f a·*dzoo*·ro/a *(light) blue*

B

bagaglio in eccedenza ba·*ga*·lyo een e·che·*den*·tsa *excess baggage*
bagaglio m ba·*ga*·lyo *luggage*
bagaglio consentito ba·*ga*·lyo kon·sen·*tee*·to *baggage allowance*
bagno m *ba*·nyo *bath • bathroom*
bambino/a m/f bam·*bee*·no/a *child*
Bancomat m *ban*·ko·mat *automatic teller machine (ATM)*
barca f *bar*·ka *boat*
bebé m&f be·*be* *baby*
bello/a m/f *be*·lo/a *beautiful • handsome • good (weather)*
bere *be*·re *drink*
bevanda f be·*van*·da *drink*
biancheria f **intima** byan·ke·*ree*·a een·tee·ma *underwear*
bianco e nero *byan*·ko e *ne*·ro *B&W*
bianco/a m/f *byan*·ko/a *white*
bicicletta f bee·chee·*kle*·ta *bicycle*
biglietteria f bee·lye·te·*ree*·a *ticket office*
biglietto m bee·*lye*·to *ticket*
biglietto m **di andata e ritorno** bee·*lye*·to dee an·*da*·ta e ree·*tor*·no *return ticket*
bimbo/a m/f *beem*·bo/a *baby*
binario m bee·*na*·ryo *platform*
birra f *bee*·ra *beer*
blu bloo *blue (dark)*
bollo m **di circolazione** *bo*·lo dee cheer·ko·la·*tsyo*·ne *car registration*
borsa f *bor*·sa *bag (general)*
bottiglia f bo·*tee*·lya *bottle*

C

cabina f **telefonica** ka·*bee*·na te·le·*fo*·nee·ka *phone box*
caffè m ka·*fe* *coffee*

caldo/a m/f *kal-do/a hot*

calzini m pl *kal-tsee-nee socks*

cambiare *kam-bya-re change*

cambio m *kam-byo exchange • change*

cambio m **valuta** *kam-byo va-loo-ta currency exchange*

camera doppia *ka-me-ra do-pya double room*

camera f **da letto** *ka-me-ra da le-to bedroom*

camera f **singola** *ka-me-ra seen-go-la single room*

camicia f *ka-mee-cha shirt*

camminare *ka-mee-na-re walk*

campagna f *kam-pa-nya countryside*

cancellare *kan-che-la-re cancel*

cane m *ka-ne dog*

cappello m *ka-pe-lo hat*

cappotto m *ka-po-to coat*

carabinieri m pl *ka-ra-bee-nye-ree police (military)*

carne f *kar-ne meat*

caro/a m/f *ka-ro/a expensive*

carrozza f **ristorante** *ka-ro-tsa rees-to-ran-te dining car*

carta f *kar-ta paper*

carta f **d'identità** *kar-ta dee-den-tee-ta identification card (ID)*

carta f **d'imbarco** *kar-ta deem-bar-ko boarding pass*

carta f **di credito** *kar-ta dee kre-dee-to credit card*

cartolaio m *kar-to-la-yo stationer*

cartolina f *kar-to-lee-na postcard*

cassiere/a m/f *ka-sye-re/a cashier*

cattivo/a m/f *ka-tee-vo/a bad*

celibe m *che-lee-be single (man)*

cellulare m *che-loo-la-re mobile phone*

cena f *che-na dinner*

centro m **commerciale** *chen-tro ko-mer-cha-le shopping centre*

cerotti m pl *che-ro-tee Band-aids*

chi *kee who*

chiave f *kya-ve key*

chiuso/a m/f *kyoo-zo/a closed • shut • locked*

ciascuno/a m/f *chas-koo-no/a each*

cintura f **di sicurezza** *cheen-too-ra dee see-koo-re-tsa seatbelt*

circo m *cheer-ko circus*

città f *chee-ta city*

classe f **business** *kla-se beez-nes business class*

classe f **turistica** *kla-se too-ree-stee-ka economy class*

collant f pl *ko-lant pantyhose*

commedia f *ko-me-dya play (theatre)*

comodo/a m/f *ko-mo-do/a comfortable*

compagno/a m/f *kom-pa-nyo/a companion • partner (intimate)*

compleanno m *kom-ple-a-no birthday*

completo/a m/f *kom-ple-to/a booked out*

comprare *kom-pra-re buy*

compreso/a m/f *kom-pre-zo/a included*

computer m *kom-pyoo-ter computer*

condividere *kon-dee-vee-de-re share (with)*

confermare *kon-fer-ma-re confirm (a booking)*

confine m *kon-fee-ne border*

congelato/a m/f *kon-je-la-to/a frozen*

conto m *kon-to bill (account)*

conto m **in banca** *kon-to een ban-ka bank account*

convalidare *kon-va-lee-da-re validate*

coperta f *ko-per-ta blanket*

coperto m *ko-per-to cover charge (restaurant)*

cucina f *koo-chee-na kitchen*

cucinare *koo-chee-na-re cook*

cuoco/a m/f *kwo-ko/a cook • chef (restaurant)*

cuoio m *kwo-yo leather*

cuscino m *koo-shee-no pillow*

D

data f **di nascita** *da·*ta dee *na·*shee·ta *date of birth*

deposito m de·*po·*zee·to *deposit (bank)*

deposito m **bagagli** de·*po·*zee·to ba·*ga·*lyee *left luggage (office)*

diapositiva f dee·a·po·zee·*tee·*va *slide (film)*

dimensioni f pl dee·men·*syo·*nee *size (general)*

diretto/a m/f dee·*re·*to/a *direct*

distributore m **automatico di biglietti** dees·tree·boo·*to·*re ow·to·*ma·*tee·ko dee bee·*lye·*tee *ticket machine*

distributore m **di servizio** dees·tree·boo·*to·*re dee ser·*vee·*tsyo *petrol station • service station*

dito m *dee·*to *finger*

doccia f *do·*cha *shower*

dogana f do·*ga·*na *customs*

domani do·*ma·*nee *tomorrow*

domani mattina do·*ma·*nee ma·*tee·*na *tomorrow morning*

domani pomeriggio do·*ma·*nee po·me·*ree·*jo *tomorrow afternoon*

domani sera do·*ma·*nee *se·*ra *tomorrow evening*

dopodomani do·po·do·*ma·*nee *day after tomorrow*

dormire dor·*mee·*re *sleep*

dove *do·*ve *where*

drogheria f dro·ge·*ree·*a *grocery*

E

edicola f e·*dee·*ko·la *newsagency*

edificio m e·dee·*fee·*cho *building*

elenco m **telefonico** e·*len·*ko te·le·*fo·*nee·ko *phone book*

entrare en·*tra·*re *enter*

entrata f en·*tra·*ta *entry*

erba f *er·*ba *grass • pot (dope)*

esposizione f es·po·zee·*tsyo·*ne *exhibition*

espresso/a m/f es·*pre·*so/a *express*

est m est *east*

estate f es·*ta·*te *summer*

F

fagioli m pl fa·*jo·*lee *beans*

famiglia f fa·*mee·*lya *family*

fantastico/a m/f fan·*tas·*tee·ko/a *great*

farmacia f far·ma·*chee·*a *pharmacy*

federa f *fe·*de·ra *pillowcase*

figlia f *fee·*lya *daughter*

figlio m *fee·*lyo *son*

finestra f fee·*nes·*tra *window (general)*

finestrino m fee·nes·*tree·*no *window (car, plane)*

foresta f fo·*res·*ta *forest*

fra poco fra *po·*ko *soon*

francobollo m fran·ko·*bo·*lo *stamp*

fratello m fra·*te·*lo *brother*

freno m *fre·*no *brake*

fresco/a m/f *fres·*ko/a *fresh*

fumare foo·*ma·*re *smoke*

G

galleria f **d'arte** ga·le·*ree·*a *dar·*te *art gallery*

gas m gaz *gas (for cooking)*

gentile jen·*tee·*le *kind • nice (person)*

giacca f *ja·*ka *jacket*

giallo/a m/f *ja·*lo/a *yellow*

giardino m jar·*dee·*no *garden*

gioielli m pl jo·ye·*lee *jewellery*

giornale m jor·*na·*le *newspaper*

giorno m *jor·*no *day*

gita f *jee*-ta tour • trip
gonna f *go*-na skirt
grande *gran*-de big • large
grande magazzino m *gran*-de
ma-ga-*dzee*-no department store
gratuito/a m/f gra-*too*-ee-to/a free
(gratis) • com pl imentary (free)
grigio/a m/f *gree*-jo/a grey
gruppo sanguigno *groo*-po
san-*gwee*-nyo blood group
guanti m *gwan*-tee gloves
guardaroba m gwar-da-*ro*-ba cloakroom

I

ieri *ye*-ree yesterday
in fondo een *fon*-do at the bottom •
after all
in lista d'attesa een *lee*-stada-*te*-za
standby (ticket)
in ritardo (adv) een ree-*tar*-do late
incidente m een-chee-*den*-te accident
influenza f een-floo-*en*-tsa flu • influenza
informazioni f pl een-for-ma-*tsyo*-nee
information
inglese een-*gle*-ze English
insieme een-*sye*-me together
Internet (point) m een-*ter*-net (poynt)
Internet (cafe)
interprete m/f een-*ter*-pre-te interpreter
intervallo m een-ter-*va*-lo intermission
inverno m een-*ver*-no winter
itinerario m ee-tee-ne-*ra*-ryo itinerary •
route

J

jeans m pl jeens jeans

L

lana f *la*-na wool
latte m *la*-te milk
lavanderia la-van-de-*ree*-a laundry (room)
lavanderia a gettone la-van-de-*ree*-a a
je-*to*-ne laundrette
lavare la-*va*-re wash (something)
lavarsi la-*var*-see wash (oneself)
lavatrice f la-va-*tree*-che washing machine
Lei pol lay you (polite)
lettera f *le*-te-ra letter
letto m *le*-to bed
letto matrimoniale *le*-to
ma-tree-mo-*nya*-le double bed
libreria f lee-bre-*ree*-a bookshop
libretto di circolazione lee-*bre*-to dee
cheer-ko-la-*tsyo*-ne car owner's title
libro m *lee*-bro book
linea aerea *lee*-ne-a a-e-re-a airline
Loro pl pol *lo*-ro you
luna di miele *loo*-na dee *mye*-le
honeymoon

M

macchina f *ma*-kee-na car • machine
macchina fotografica *ma*-kee-na
fo-to-*gra*-fee-ka camera
macelleria f ma-che-le-*ree*-a butcher's shop
madre f *ma*-dre mother
maglione m ma-*lyo*-ne jumper • sweater
mancia f *man*-cha tip (gratuity)
mangiare man-*ja*-re eat
marciapiede m mar-cha-*pye*-de footpath
mare m *ma*-re sea
marrone m/f ma-*ro*-ne brown
mattina f ma-*tee*-na morning
medicina f me-dee-*chee*-na medicine
medico m *me*-dee-ko doctor

menù m me-*noo* menu
mercato m mer-*ka*-to market
mese m *me*-ze month
mezzanotte f me-dza-*no*-te midnight
mezzo m *me*-dzo half
moda f *mo*-da fashion
modem m *mo*-dem modem
moglie f *mo*-lye wife
montagna f mon-*ta*-nya mountain
mostrare mos-*tra*-re show
multa f *mool*-ta fine (payment)
musica f *moo*-zee-ka music

N

Natale m na-*ta*-le Christmas
negozio m ne-*go*-tsyo shop
nero/a m/f *ne*-ro/a black
neve f *ne*-ve snow
no no *no*
noleggiare no-le-*ja*-re hire
nome m *no*-me name
non non *no* • not
non fumatore non foo-ma-*to*-re nonsmoking
nord m nord north
notte f *no*-te night
nubile f *noo*-bee-le single (woman)
numero m *noo*-me-ro number
numero m **di camera** *noo*-me-ro dee *ka*-me-ra room number
nuotare nwo-*ta*-re swim

O

occhiali m pl o-*kya*-lee glasses (spectacles)
oggi *o*-jee today
olio m *o*-lyo oil
ora f *o*-ra hour
orario m o-*ra*-ryo timetable
orario m **di apertura** o-*ra*-ryo dee a-per-*too*-ra opening hours

oro m *o*-ro gold
ospedale m os-pe-*da*-le hospital
ostello m **della gioventù** os-*te*-lo de-la jo-ven-*too* youth hostel
ovest m *o*-vest west

P

padre m *pa*-dre father
pagamento m pa-ga-*men*-to payment
palazzo m pa-*la*-tso palace
pane m *pa*-ne bread
panetteria f pa-ne-te-*ree*-a bakery
pannolino m pa-no-*lee*-no diaper • nappy
pantaloni m pl pan-ta-*lo*-nee pants • trousers
parrucchiere m pa-roo-*kye*-re beauty salon
partenza f par-*ten*-tsa departure
partire par-*tee*-re depart • leave
passaporto m pa-sa-*por*-to passport
passeggero/a m/f pa-se-*je*-ro/a passenger
passeggiata f pa-se-*ja*-ta walk
pasticceria f pa-stee-che-*ree*-a cake shop
pasto m *pas*-to meal
patente f **(di guida)** pa-*ten*-te (deegwee-da) drivers licence
pellicola f pe-*lee*-ko-la film (for camera)
penna f **(a sfera)** *pe*-na (a *sfe*-ra) pen (ballpoint)
pensionato/a m/f pen-syo-*na*-to/a pensioner • retired
perché per-*ke* why • because
perso/a m/f *per*-so/a lost
pescheria f pe-ske-*ree*-a fish shop
pezzo m **di antiquariato** *pe*-tso dee an-tee-kwa-*rya*-to antique
piano m *pya*-no floor (storey)
picnic m *peek*-neek picnic
pila f *pee*-la battery
piscina f pee-*shee*-na swimming pool
pittore/pittrice m/f pee-*to*-re/ pee-*tree*-che painter
pittura f pee-*too*-ra painting (the art)

polizia f po·lee·*tsee*·a police (civilian)
pomeriggio m po·me·*ree*·jo afternoon
portacenere m por·ta·*che*·ne·re ashtray
portatile m por·*ta*·tee·le laptop
posta f *pos*·ta mail
posta f ordinaria *pos*·ta or·dee·*na*·rya surface mail
posta f prioritaria *pos*·ta pree·o·ree·*ta*·rya express mail
posteggio m di tassì po·*ste*·jo dee ta·*see* taxi stand
posto m di polizia *pos*·to dee po·lee·*tsee*·a police station
pranzo m *pran*·dzo lunch
prenotare pre·no·*ta*·re book (make a booking)
preservativo m pre·zer·va·*tee*·vo condom
presto m/f *pres*·to early
prezzo m *pre*·tso price
prima classe f *pree*·ma *kla*·se first class
prima colazione f *pree*·ma ko·la·*tsyo*·ne breakfast
primavera f *pree*·ma·*ve*·ra spring (season)
prossimo/a m/f *pro*·see·mo/a next
pulce f *pool*·che flea
pulito/a m/f poo·*lee*·to/a clean
pulizia f poo·lee·*tsee*·a cleaning
pullman m *pool*·man bus (coach)

Q

quadro m *kwa*·dro painting (canvas)
quando *kwan*·do when
qui kwee here

R

raccomandata f ra·ko·man·*da*·ta registered mail
ragazza f ra·*ga*·tsa girl(friend)
ragazzo m ra·*ga*·tso boy(friend)
regalo m re·*ga*·lo present (gift)

reggiseno m re·jee·se·no bra
registrazione f re·jee·stra·*tsyo*·ne check-in (hotel)
resto m *res*·to change (money)
ricetta f ree·*che*·ta prescription
ricevuta f ree·che·*voo*·ta receipt
rimborso m reem·*bor*·so refund
riparare ree·pa·*ra*·re repair
ritardo m ree·*tar*·do delay
ritiro m bagagli ree·*tee*·ro ba·*ga*·lyee baggage claim
ritorno m ree·*tor*·no return
rosa m/f *ro*·za pink
rosso/a m/f *ro*·so/a red
rotto/a m/f *ro*·to/a broken
rubato/a m/f roo·*ba*·to/a stolen

S

sacchetto m sa·*ke*·to bag (shopping)
sacco a pelo *sa*·ko a *pe*·lo sleeping bag
sala di transito *sa*·la dee *tran*·zee·to transit lounge
sala f d'attesa *sa*·la da·*te*·za waiting room
salumeria f sa·loo·me·*ree*·a delicatessen
salva slip m pl *sal*·va·*sleep* panty liners
sarto/a m/f *sar*·to/a tailor
scale f pl *ska*·le stairway
scarpe f pl *skar*·pe shoes
scatola f *ska*·to·la box • carton • tin
scheda f telefonica *ske*·da te·le·*fo*·nee·ka phone card
schiena f *skye*·na back (body)
sconto m *skon*·to discount
secco/a m/f *se*·ko/a dry
sedile m se·*dee*·le seat (chair)
seggiovia f se·jo·*vee*·a chairlift (skiing)
sentiero m sen·*tye*·ro path • track • trail
senza *sen*·tsa without
servizio m ser·*vee*·tsyo service • service charge
settimana f se·tee·*ma*·na week

sicuro/a m/f see-*koo*-ro/a *safe*
sigaretta f see-ga-*re*-ta *cigarette*
soccorso m so-*kor*-so *help • aid*
soldi m pl *sol*-dee *money • cash*
solo andata f *so*-lo an-*da*-ta *one-way*
sorella f so-*re*-la *sister*
spiaggia f *spya*-ja *beach*
sporco/a m/f *spor*-ko/a *dirty*
spuntino m spoon-*tee*-no *snack*
stagione f sta-*jo*-ne *season*
stanza f *stan*-tsa *room*
stazione della metropolitana sta-*tsyo*-ne *de*-la me-tro-po-lee-*ta*-na *metro station*
stazione f **d'autobus** sta-*tsyo*-ne *dow*-to-boos *bus station*
stazione f **ferroviaria** sta-*tsyo*-ne fe-ro-*vyar*-ya *train station*
sterlina f ster-*lee*-na *pound (money)*
straniero/a m/f stra-*nye*-ro/a *foreign*
studente/studentessa m/f stoo-*den*-te/ stoo-den-*te*-sa *student*
sud m sood *south*
suocera f *swo*-che-ra *mother-in-law*
supermercato m soo-per-mer-*ka*-to *supermarket*
sveglia f *sve*-lya *alarm clock*

T

tardi *tar*-dee *late*
temperino m tem-pe-*ree*-no *penknife*
tossire to-*see*-re *cough*
traghetto m tra-*ge*-to *ferry*
trucco m *troo*-ko *make-up*
tu too *you (inf)*
tutto m *too*-to *everything*

U

ubriaco/a m/f oo-bree-*a*-ko/a *drunk*
ufficio m oo-*fee*-cho *office*

ufficio m **del turismo** oo-*fee*-cho del too-*reez*-mo *tourist office*
ufficio m **oggetti smarriti** o-*je*-tee sma-*ree*-tee *lost property office*
ufficio m **postale** oo-*fee*-cho pos-*ta*-le *post office*
ultimo/a m/f *ool*-tee-mo/a *last*
uomo m *wo*-mo *man*
uscire con oo-*shee*-re kon *go out with • date*
uscita f oo-*shee*-ta *exit*

V

vacanze f pl va-*kan*-tse *holidays*
vagone m **letto** va-*go*-ne *le*-to *sleeping car*
valigetta f va-lee-*je*-ta *briefcase*
veloce ve-*lo*-che *fast*
verde *ver*-de *green*
verdura f ver-*doo*-ra *vegetable*
via f **aerea** *vee*-a a-*e*-re-a *airmail*
viaggio m **d'affari** *vya*-jo da-*fa*-ree *business trip*
videoregistratore m vee-de-o-re-jee-str a-*to*-re *video*
vino m *vee*-no *wine*
viola *vee*-o-la *purple*
visita f **guidata** *vee*-see-ta gwee-*da*-ta *guided tour*
vista f *vee*-sta *view*
vocabolarietto m vo-ka-bo-la-*rye*-to *phrasebook*
vocabolario m vo-ka-bo-*la*-ryo *dictionary*
volo m *vo*-lo *flight*

Z

zaino m *dzai*-no *backpack • knapsack*
zia f *tsee*-a *aunt*

A

abbreviations	12
accidents	68
accommodation	61
addresses	15, 53
admission	22
age	18
air-conditioning	64
allergies	40, 73
apologies	13
appointments	34
art	21
ATM	49

B

baggage	57
banks	49, 50
bargaining	29
bars	39
Basilica di San Marco, La	26
bed & breakfast accommodation	61
beliefs	19
bill (accommodation)	63
bill (restaurant)	36
boat	54
booking (tickets)	55
booking (accommodation)	62
booking (restaurant)	35
booking (transport)	56
books	31
bookshops	30
breakfast	35
bus	54, 57
business	67
business cards	66
business equipment	67
buying food	39
buying things	27

C

camping ground	61
car hire	59
CDs	31

cell phones	51
changing money	50
checking email	52
checking in (accommodation)	62
checking out (accommodation)	65
chemist	70
Chianti	24
cinema	33
clothes	30
clubs	33
coffee styles	38
collect calls	51
Colosseum	25
colours	74
compass points	54
complaints (accommodation)	64
conditions (medical)	71
conferences	66
consulates	70
conversation	34
credit cards	29
crime	69

D

dates	75
day trips	24
days of the week	75
debit cards	29
dentists	70
diets	40, 41
dining out	35
dinner	35
directions	53
discounts	29
doctors	70
drinks (alcoholic)	38, 39
drinks (nonalcoholic)	37
drugs (medical)	70

E

eateries	36
eating out	35
email	52
embassies	70

emergencies 68
emotions 19
employment 17
entertainment 33
essential language 13
exchanging goods 28

F

fax 49
feelings 18
film (photographic) 32
Florence 24, 25
food 35

G

galleries 21
gas (petrol) 60
gay venues 33
going out 33
greetings 13
guidebooks 20
guided tours 22
guide (tourist) 20, 23

H

health 70, 73
hotels 61

I

illnesses 72
injuries 71
internet 52
interpreters 67
Italian language facts 12

L

language difficulties 16
Leaning Tower of Pisa 25
lost possessions 69
Lucca 24

luggage 57
lunch 35

M

mail 49
medical conditions 72
medical needs 70
medication 73
meeting 34
meetings (business) 66
meeting people 13
meeting up 34
menu items 42, 48
menu terms 41
metro 57
Milan 26
mobile phones 51
motorbike hire 59
museums 21
music 30, 31, 31

N

Naples 25
non-smoking section (restaurant) 35
non-smoking section (transport) 56
numbers 74

O

occupations 17
ordering food 36
Ostia Antica 24

P

parcels 49
paying for things 29
petrol 60
pharmacy 70
phone 50
phone numbers 15
photography 21, 32
police 69

police station 69
Pompeii 25
Ponte Vecchio 26
post office 49
prescriptions 73

R

rates (mobile phone) 51
reading 30
receipts 29
refunds 29
religion 19
repairs 30
requests (accommodation) 63, 65
responses (invitations) 34
restaurants 35
returning goods 28
reverse-charges call 51
road signs 60
Rome 24

S

Scala, La 26
seasons 76
shoes 30
shopping 27
shopping precincts 28
Siena 24
sightseeing 20
SIM card 52
sizes 30
small talk 34
snack 35
specialities 39
speed limit 60
stolen possessions 69
studies 18
symptoms 71

T

taxi 58, 59
telephone 50, 51
theft 69
tickets (transport) 55, 56
titles 13
Tivoli 24
toilets 68
tours 22
train 54, 58
transport 54, 55
travellers cheques 29, 50

U

Uffizi, Gli 26

V

vaccinations 71
Vatican city 25
vegan food 41
vegetarian food 40, 41
Venice 26

W

weather 19
wine 39
work 66

Y

youth hostels 61

NOTES

don't just stand there, say something!

To see the full range of our language products, go to:
lonelyplanet.com

What kind of traveller are you?

A. You're eating chicken for dinner *again* because it's the only word you know.

B. When no one understands what you say, you step closer and shout louder.

C. When the barman doesn't understand your order, you point frantically at the beer.

D. You're surrounded by locals, swapping jokes, email addresses and experiences – other travellers want to borrow your phrasebook or audio guide.

If you answered A, B, or C, you NEED Lonely Planet's language products ...

- **Lonely Planet Phrasebooks** – for every phrase you need in every language you want
- **Lonely Planet Language & Culture** – get behind the scenes of English as it's spoken around the world – learn and laugh
- **Lonely Planet Fast Talk & Fast Talk Audio** – essential phrases for short trips and weekends away – read, listen and talk like a local
- **Lonely Planet Small Talk** – 10 essential languages for city breaks
- **Lonely Planet Real Talk** – downloadable language audio guides from lonelyplanet.com to your MP3 player

... and this is why

- **Talk to everyone everywhere**
  Over 120 languages, more than any other publisher
- **The right words at the right time**
  Quick-reference colour sections, two-way dictionary, easy pronunciation, every possible subject – and audio to support it

Lonely Planet Offices

Australia
90 Maribyrnong St, Footscray,
Victoria 3011
☎ 03 8379 8000
fax 03 8379 8111
✉ talk2us@lonelyplanet.com.au

USA
150 Linden St, Oakland,
CA 94607
☎ 510 893 8555
fax 510 893 8572
✉ info@lonelyplanet.com

UK
72-82 Rosebery Ave,
London EC1R 4RW
☎ 020 7841 9000
fax 020 7841 9001
✉ go@lonelyplanet.co.uk

lonelyplanet.com